"*Done is Better Tha* practical advice an building a profitable wedding business. A must-read for anyone looking to thrive in the wedding industry."

*Meghan Ely – Wedding Publicist, OFD Consulting*

"From starting out to scaling up, Becca's book is packed with practical advice and actionable steps for your wedding business, empowering you to tackle challenges with confidence."

*Nikita Thorne – Head of Strategy, Guides for Brides*

Dear Braden!
My book is less sweary than yours :)
. Love you more than the crack shack
x Becca x

# DONE IS BETTER THAN PERFECT

# BECCA POUNTNEY

DONE
DONE
DONE
DONE
# DONE
# IS BETTER
# THAN
# PERFECT

Building a profitable
wedding business

First published in 2024 by BP Publishing

ISBN (Paperback): 978-1-3999-9584-9
ISBN (eBook): 978-1-0369-0000-7

Printed and bound in the United Kingdom

Cover design by Hannah Beatrice Owens

Copy-editing by Mary Davis Editing

## Thanks

To my family – thanks for putting up with me throughout this book writing process and always loving me even when I am not perfect.

To my parents – thanks for raising me to believe that anything is possible.

To every wedding pro and wedding venue that I have ever worked with – you are the reason that I do what I do. Thanks for your kind words and encouragements along the journey.

# CONTENTS

**Introduction:** The accidental entrepreneur    7

1   **Being business-like:** Make it official    19

2   **Preparing for success:** Get out of your own way    33

3   **Your offer:** Build your brand    55

4   **Marketing:** Start the puzzle    77

5   **Simplify:** Untangle your processes    121

6   **Sales:** Close the deal    137

7   **Relationships:** Being friends with everyone    165

8   **Facing the numbers:** Becoming profitable    187

**Final thoughts**    203

**Work with me**    205

# INTRO-DUCTION
The accidental entrepreneur

'What qualifies you to talk about wedding businesses,' said the voice across the table at dinner.

I took a big gulp of my drink.

The pause before I thought of what to say felt like ten minutes although it was probably only ten seconds. My brain was spinning as I tried to formulate some kind of answer.

I had just spoken on stage at a huge international wedding event, the feedback on my talk was positive and I knew people would make leaps forward in their businesses based on the things I had shared. Why was this question over dinner causing me so much panic? I shuffled awkwardly through an answer, reeling off my years of experience, my background in television and radio, and stories of the countless wedding businesses I've helped to grow in confidence and profit over the last eight years. Eventually, the conversation moved on – but I didn't.

## Something to prove?

As I wandered back to my hotel room that evening, I pondered this scenario. Why did I feel I had something to prove to this stranger? Were they hoping I would produce a degree certificate in Wedding Industry Education out of my handbag? What is it that proves we are 'qualified' to own and run our own businesses?

When I look back over my own journey, I realise that I became an 'accidental entrepreneur'. I didn't sit down one day and write a huge business plan to get me to where I am today. Each little step on my life path has led me to this moment. My years working in television and radio taught me so much about how big brands approach their marketing. My time owning a wedding videography company showed me how the wedding industry works. And my own life experience has led me to a place where I can use all those things to help other people.

The results speak for themselves – the reviews and testimonials, the clients who have quit their day jobs to be full-time, or those that listen to my training and find little moments of inspiration to take their business to the next level.

There is no simple answer to, 'What qualifies you, Becca?' It's a huge, lifelong journey. I don't need to justify myself to a stranger over dinner – and neither do you.

*'Done is better than perfect.'*

'Done is better than perfect' is a phrase I have used frequently over the last eight years with wedding business owners – or 'wedding pros' as I call them. Anyone who has had the confidence to start a business needs to remember it – whether you're a florist, caterer, DJ, wedding venue owner, wedding planner or any of the hundreds of businesses involved in the wedding industry.

As I have interviewed many, many wedding pros on my podcast about their journey to success, one thing has become clear, I'm not the only accidental entrepreneur in the wedding industry and there certainly isn't a one-size-fits-all wedding industry degree that people take to find success.

From the hobbyist photographer who got asked to take photos for a friend's wedding and now works full time in the industry to the pianist who started making musical TikToks and now records ceremony music and first dance songs for couples worldwide – everyone has their own background and stories to tell. They all had a moment where they wondered what qualified them to do this job that they love.

## Doing what we love

Why wouldn't you want to be doing a job you love?

There is something about society that teaches us from a young age that 'work' is hard, boring and even something to be hated. We should 'look forward to the weekend' and be miserable on Sunday evening because we have to go back to work on Monday.

Surely there's a better way? Why shouldn't you make money and enjoy the work you do? Why can't you have fun doing what you love and making money from it.

Loving your work doesn't make it a hobby. The happiest people I know have worked out how to turn that hobby they have into a profitable business. Not only do they find joy in what they do, they can also create an income for themselves and their family too.

*Why wouldn't you want to be doing a job you love?*

When I booked a flight to Las Vegas to go to the world's biggest wedding industry conference, my friends made jokes.

'That's not work,' they said, 'that's just a holiday.'

'Well,' I said, 'maybe when you love your work, it can be both.'

I'm pretty sure, if they had that opportunity, they would seize it with both hands. So why shouldn't I? Why shouldn't you?

If you have a passion or a creative spark, you absolutely have the opportunity to turn it into a business. Your personal experience and talent has brought you to this place and now it's time to turn that passion into a profitable business that you love.

The wedding industry is a magical community to be part of, with everyone working together to create happiness and lasting memories for couples on what will likely be one of the best days of their lives. We work hard, there are late nights, long days and you will wear all sorts of hats, but the moment you see that couple smiling on the wedding day, it all becomes worth it.

When I stepped off the stage after speaking at a conference last year, one of the attendees came bounding over to me and enthusiastically asked me where she could purchase a copy of my book. I stared blankly at her. 'I don't have a book,' I replied. 'Well, you should!' she replied.

## Done is better than perfect

In that moment, I doubted myself. Could I ever write a book? I am no wordsmith and I definitely never dreamt of becoming an author. As I reflected over the coming days, I remembered that phrase again: done is better than perfect. If I can share my knowledge and help just one business owner with my writing, it will be worth it. This book is an imperfect guide – because as humans we are all full of imperfection. There are certainly more polished authors out there, but I've learnt that waiting until I'm perfect often means missing opportunities. So, I'm taking my own advice and sharing my knowledge with you, even though it's not flawless.

I hope this book becomes your companion and trusted advisor, perhaps even your secret weapon. You know you are good at the creative part – planning the wedding, arranging the flowers, taking the video or baking the cake. Now let's make sure you have the business side of things under control as well.

## Your unique skills

I can't make a cake. My friends and family know me to be a disaster in the kitchen. (I was even advised to drop cooking at school after I set fire to a pan of boiling spaghetti.) The closest I get to arranging flowers is cutting the stems off the bottom of my supermarket-bought flowers. I can't take great photos or write a ceremony. I'm not great at styling a venue or getting a crowd on a dance floor.

But what I do know is how to create, market and sell a successful wedding business. So, let's work together. You bring your skill and I will bring my knowledge through this book – and together we can create you a profitable successful business, doing what you love.

## Glossary of terms

Before we dive in, I want to share some 'Becca-isms' with you to make the process of reading this book easier. There are some topics that I will refer to throughout the book, so I've listed them here for your reference.

If you scan the QR code at the end of this section, you will find all the links mentioned in the book. As a bonus, there's also a link to two of my Spotify playlists for anyone who loves 1990's pop and musical theatre as much as I do… You're welcome!

### MY PODCAST

My podcast is called 'Wedding Pros who are Ready to Grow' and you can listen to it on any of the major podcast apps or directly on my website. I chat to a mixture of wedding pros and industry experts as well as share my own marketing advice with you. Think of it as a little weekly dose of wedding business inspiration.

## THE MEMBERS LOUNGE

This is my paid-for community of wedding professionals and venue owners. It's also my personal business safe space online. It's where you can stay accountable, stay ahead with your learning, and collaborate and learn from some of the most amazing people in the wedding industry. It's a place where you can rant, celebrate your wins or be vulnerable about your struggles with other people who get it. We get together online and in person and we welcome everyone. You have to be part of it to truly understand its value.

## WEDDING PROS

This is how I refer to anyone who is working in and around the wedding industry. Whether you are a business owner, a venue owner or an employee of a wedding business or venue – this is you! I love the term 'Wedding Pro', because we are pros at doing weddings.

## IMPERFECTION

As humans, we will never be perfect, so this describes every one of us. Stop being held back by perfectionism and embrace being perfectly imperfect!

## THE SPICE GIRLS

Quite frankly, the best 1990's pop band there ever was. They were my heroes as a child, and musically I haven't really moved on. I celebrate Girl Power, adopt their signature peace sign and generally just light up if I hear their music. Deep down I always wanted to be a Spice Girl, so I talk about them regularly.

## DISNEYWORLD

This is the deep-rooted 'why' of my business. I'm sure I am supposed to have a bigger backstory but, other than work that fits around my children, Disney is probably up there as one of my biggest 'whys'. When you choose to work with me, the chances are that your money is going towards my next family visit to the happiest place on earth. I also love to learn lessons from Disney. They are incredible at customer service and customer experience, and I think we can learn a lot from a trip to Florida.

## MY FAMILY

I will probably refer to my family at times in this book. I am married and have two children, who are ten and seven at the time of writing. The elder is Mr Musical and the sensible one who already knows more about technology than I do. The younger is Miss Football Mad and has an inner confidence we could all learn from.

## MUSICAL THEATRE

I *love* musical theatre. It's an escape for me. Whether watching a show, singing along in the shower or performing on stage, it brings me *so* much joy. I find musical theatre can be like Marmite – so you may love it or hate it. I'm sure there will be the occasional niche musical theatre reference in my writing – see if you can spot them.

So now that's all out of the way, let's start at the very beginning...[1]

---

1   Yes, this is the first shameless musical theatre reference. It's from *The Sound of Music* (if you were wondering).

1

# BEING BUSINESS-LIKE

Make it official

This is the chapter I was least looking forward to writing… because it's the bit of business I don't enjoy. As an entrepreneur, my tendency is to jump right into the fun and creative ideas – but, realistically, these foundations are important when it comes to creating a profitable, sustainable business.

So we are going to 'Eat That Frog' and do the hard bit first, because then it will all feel easier from here.[1] A word of warning. There are people much more qualified to write this chapter than I am. However, I am going to write this in a way that I wish someone had written for me – simple and straightforward. Sometimes people make 'business' sound much harder than it is, when all we really need is a basic explanation.

These are the steps that I followed in setting up my own business. However, every business is unique, so please make sure you consult a professional advisor about the specific requirements of your business to ensure you're on the right track.

I remember sitting down with my friend just after we had decided to launch our wedding videography business. We had watched one too many episodes of Dragons' Den (known as the Shark Tank in the USA) and thought, 'Why not us?'

We had a planning meeting over a cup of tea and decided we would start a business... but then realised we were not too sure what happened next. How do you actually start a business? After a lot of googling and

---

1    Brian Tracy, *Eat That Frog! Get More Of The Important Things Done Today* (Yellow Kite, 2013).

getting things wrong, we eventually worked it out, and it really was much simpler than we thought.

I like breaking things down into manageable chunks – so here are some things you need to do to get you on the way to becoming an 'official' business owner.

## 1. Declare yourself a business owner

Here in the UK, you don't actually have to register your business (unless you want to be a limited company). For most of you, you can just contact HMRC and let them know you want to register to be a Sole Trader.[2] This essentially means you declare your additional income so that you pay the right tax. You can earn this money from various different sources, but it all gets declared in one place. For example, you may already have a full-

*We need these essential steps in place to ensure we have a solid business foundation to build on.*

or part-time job, in which case, you would declare your wedding business income in addition. Perhaps you only have your wedding business but do some extra work on the side as a Virtual Assistant. All the income comes in to you and you declare it in your Self-Assessment.

---

2  If you search the internet for 'HMRC sole trader', you will find lots of relevant information.

If you decide to go into business with someone else (as I did originally), it is slightly more complicated as you will need to register as a Partnership. If this is you, then get some more formal advice on how to do this correctly. Whenever you go into partnership with anyone, you need to have lots of ground rules and agreements between yourselves to stop the relationship going sour.

Whether you're a sole trader or in a partnership, you need to do this straight away. Don't wait until you start making money. You want to have a clear start date registered and to have everything above board from day one. The great news is you won't pay any tax until you make a profit, but having this job done from the start is well worth it.

If you are based outside the UK, then your tax rules and business registration guidelines will vary. Chat with fellow wedding pros or educators in your country who I am sure will be able to help.

## 2. Buy a domain name

It turns out that a domain and a website are not the same thing. Before owning a business, I didn't understand this, so although this may be basic, I'm speaking to those of you that may not know the difference. A domain name is just the website address and usually costs around £20 per year (unless it's a highly sought-after address). There are websites that show you which domain names are available to purchase and how much they are going to cost.[3] It's worth trying to secure your domain name early in the process before finalising your business name. You don't want to spend hours on logos to then find your desired website domain isn't available – because then it's back to the drawing board.

When I worked in radio, I learnt early on that a clear, concise domain name is important. A radio ad doesn't work if your domain name doesn't make sense when being read out loud. If it's too long and complicated, nobody will remember it. If a radio advert said, 'Find out more from us by visiting www.beccasweddings-business.com/home/bookme/12345', it would be completely useless.

Keep it clear, short and snappy and read it out loud to make sure it works.

## 3. Secure your social media handles

This may seem a premature step, but in the social media society we live in, this is becoming an ever-important step. If you want people to find you everywhere, you need to make sure you can be found everywhere for the same thing. I lose count of the people I speak to who say their business is called beccaswedding.com but on Instagram they are bwedding1234 because the handle @beccas-wedding wasn't available. It's a clunky way to market

---

3   I have used domains.squarespace.com.

yourself and just makes it one step harder for your clients to find you.

When you check your domain is available, go and check the key social media accounts and grab the usernames straight away. You don't need to post anything yet, but knowing you have the handle secured will make your marketing much easier. I also recommend doing a quick search on social media sites of your business name idea, in case there are already lots of businesses with the same (or similar) name out there. You don't want people to go elsewhere when they are looking for you, so look for something unique that stands out from the crowd.

You would be surprised how many wedding businesses have names that sound the same as each other. Don't use all the clichéd language. Either use your name or something out of the box that sets you apart from the crowd. It will help people remember you.

## 4. Build a basic website

'Don't start your business on borrowed land,' I heard one of my business mentors say. Social media doesn't belong to you and they can take it away at any moment. I sat with that thought for a while. What did he mean?

Just a few days later, one of my clients was hacked and they lost their Instagram account. I saw the ground fall from beneath their feet. Their years of content and contacts had gone in an instant and suddenly what that business mentor said made sense. Social media is great – I will talk about it a huge amount – but ultimately it doesn't belong to you. A website and email list is a much more secure option and it belongs to you. So, make sure you have one from day one.

I like to describe your social media accounts as shop windows. They are there to showcase your work and entice people in. Your website is the shop – this is where the transaction happens and where people come to buy. A shop window without a shop is useless.

A basic website is an essential part of your business – not only does it build trust with your potential clients, it also allows you to be found on Google. Let's be honest, we all still go to search engines to find services and products – why wouldn't you want to be there?

Websites are no longer something that can only be created by someone 'techy'. Increasingly, there are platforms that allow anyone to build a simple website from scratch, with drag and drop options. Although I believe a 'professionally designed' website is an important and valuable asset, this may not be an option when you are just starting out. Get a basic website together and link it to the domain you purchased so people can find you.

Don't be overcome by perfectionism at this point. We will talk in depth in later chapters about creating a beautifully branded website. Remember that 'Done is better than perfect'. Your website can and will evolve. It can be improved over time – but having *something* is a starting point. Everyone has to start somewhere.

When was the last time you purchased something from a business that didn't have a website? A website builds a level of trust. It's easy for a business to pop up on social media overnight – but a website takes a deeper level of commitment.

A further reason that a website is a core element of your wedding business is that it will help you get found by search engines. In my house, we often say, 'Let's google it'. Google solves almost all of our problems, helps us find solutions and can answer most questions in seconds. We know couples are using search engines to help with their wedding planning, so why wouldn't you want to be part of the search results?

When it comes to your website, there are a couple of layers you need to consider: 1) the website itself and 2) the website hosting. The website is your online shop window and website hosting is the place where your website files sit to enable them to be on the internet. You need to research your options. Some website builders such as Squarespace and Showit include hosting as part of their packages.

I recommend investing in your website platform from day one. You will need to decide which platform works best for your individual requirements. When I first started out, my website was built and hosted on Squarespace, but as my business needs grew and developed I decided to move to Word Press with the 'Divi theme' and the site is now hosted with Siteground.[4]

When you purchase your domain name, I also recommend purchasing the email address to match. Although

4    showit.com, www.squarespace.com,
     wordpress.com/support/five-step-website-setup,
     www.elegantthemes.com/gallery/divi, www.siteground.co.uk.

it's an additional cost, it is much more professional to use a branded email address than a free one and will show your customers that you mean business. What will be your main email address? Do you want info@ or contact@ or yourname@?

## 5. Open a business bank account

Do this now. Don't wait until later down the line. The ultimate key to being a successful wedding business owner is ensuring you are turning a healthy profit. When it comes to your wedding business, keeping on top of the finances from day one will really help. There are online banks such as Starling here in the UK which allow you to set up a business bank account without cost. Once it's ready, ensure everything that comes in and out of your business comes through this account. Don't muddy the water by allowing your personal and business finances to become intertwined.

In my banking app, I have the facility to create spaces within the account so that I can keep money aside for larger items and tax. Moving a portion of your income into a tax space each month will make life a lot easier when it's time to pay your tax bill.

## 6. Record keeping

Ensure you are keeping records of everything coming in and out of the business. Setting up a basic spreadsheet on Google Sheets or Microsoft Excel is a good place to start. I have templates that you can use for this inside the Wedding Pro Members Lounge, but you could also create your own.

## 7. Email marketing

Email marketing is a crucial element of your business and I recommend setting up an email marketing system from day one. Although you will use your email address for day-to-day messaging, an email marketing system allows you to send mailshots to large numbers of people at once while also holding their data securely and in accordance with GDPR regulations.

I always recommend my clients start with the free version of Mailerlite as it is user-friendly and won't cost you anything when you are starting out. You can use this software to send monthly email newsletters to your customer base, follow up with leads after a wedding show or as a way to attract new leads.[5]

We will talk more about email marketing in chapter 4.

## 8. Find an accountant

For the first two years of my wedding business, I decided to file my own tax returns to save money. Looking back, I can see this was a mistake as I didn't really know what I was doing. When it comes to finding an accountant,

5    accounts.mailerlite.com.

I always recommend asking around to see who others recommend. When you use an accountant, you have two options: the cheapest option is to do your own book-keeping and then pay an accountant to file the return at the end of the process. If you want to hand it all over, then you can pay for a full service, but it will cost significantly more.

I believe hiring an accountant to file your returns actually saves you time and stress in the long run. They do this day in and day out, and the chances are your accounts are actually fairly simple. Once I'd hired Emma, my accountant, I soon realised there were tax deductions I could claim and the savings she uncovered for me actually exceeded the cost of hiring her. Not only is it better financially, but the peace of mind is also worth the investment. If the auditors come knocking, it will be her that's dealing with them and not me!

## 9. Pensions

It took me a long time to start paying into a pension, and I wish I had done it sooner as it's amazing how a small contribution can start to build. It's never too soon to start paying a regular amount into a pension to help you prepare for retirement, in fact the earlier you start the better. Speak to a pension advisor to get tailored advice, but don't be afraid of it. It's simpler than you think to get it started.

## 10. Get insured

Insurance is the item that you don't realise the true importance of until you really need it. A couple of years ago, my friend returned to her rented flat to find a fire crew outside. The flat beneath her had caught fire and pretty much everything she owned was destroyed or so smoky that it had all become unusable. It was a dreadful situation, but I remember one of the first things she said to me afterwards: 'I'm so thankful that my dad got me the best contents insurance possible.' I'm fairly sure that before the fire we had never discussed her insurance policies. But in the aftermath of an unexpected disaster, it became a crucial talking point and we were all thankful she had made that investment.

Many wedding venues will ask you to show them your insurance certificates before they allow you to work there, so speak with a good tax broker and work out what you need. Here in the UK, Public Liability Insurance is an absolute must – but depending on the services you offer, there may be other insurance requirements as well.

## 11. Get contracts in place

I've lost track of the number of conversations I have had with wedding pros who are taking bookings without a formal contract. If that is you, then you are playing a dangerous game. It's important you work out your contracts ahead of time, so that you are prepared if something goes wrong. In your contract, you need to ensure you have laid out your payment terms and your cancellation policies. It is not uncommon for couples to break up during the engagement period and if you don't have a good contract in place, you won't have a clear process to follow.

When it comes to contracts, I recommend hiring a professional to write one for you. Alternatively, there are companies that will sell you contract templates specifically for the wedding industry. This can be a lower cost option – but make sure you know what you are buying and are happy with the terms you set out. Always get clients to sign your contract at the start and have it on hand if something goes wrong. Always refer back to the contract they signed.

Adapt your contract as your business develops and you grow in experience. On my Wedding Pros Facebook group, business owners often discuss situations which may lead you to identify gaps in your contract or Terms & Conditions.

## All the ducks in a row

Phew, we made it! We have covered off the practicalities of starting your wedding business. I know it's not glamorous. However, we need these essential steps in place to ensure we have a solid business foundation to build on.

Now that you have all of your ducks in a row, it's time to dive into the fun stuff... Let's build that dream wedding business.

# PREPARING FOR SUCCESS

Get out of your own way

Last summer my football-mad daughter asked to go to football camp during the school summer break. I suggested the local camp and she looked at me straight in the eye and said, 'I was thinking I would rather go and play with Premier League team.' At the age of just six, she had big goals and big dreams, and she knew that playing in our local village was nowhere near as exciting an opportunity as learning from one of the biggest clubs in the country.

I did some research and found a Tottenham Hotspurs camp that was taking place an hour down the road and I booked her in. If you are unfamiliar with the UK football system, Tottenham Hotspurs is one of the top five biggest football clubs in the UK. On her first day of the five-day camp, she returned home with a big smile on her face and proudly announced to me that tomorrow she planned to win the Star Player of the Day Award. I did what most parents would do in this situation (rightly or wrongly) and told her that her chance of winning was low, due to the fact there were 100+ other kids at the camp. I think we make comments like this to protect our children from the big wide world out there, but she looked me right in the eye once more and said, 'Yes, but I'm one of the best.'

## I'm one of the best

Wow! If only we could all have that level of confidence in our wedding businesses. I have worked with thousands of wedding pros all over the world and had many conversations about how they don't feel good enough, how they don't feel they can charge more because they don't have the experience, or that they feel that everyone else is better than they are. Very rarely does someone tell me that they think that they are the best at what they do.

Why do we have so little belief in ourselves? What happened between the age of six and now that knocked us or made us believe that we couldn't tell people we are the best? Whenever I look at the work of someone who says they are not good enough, I am nearly always blown away by their talent. They are usually incredible at what they do, but all they can see is the imperfection.

*'Yes, but I'm one of the best.'*

Most people believe that self-confidence is critical to professional success. However, The Gitnux Market Data Report 2024 reveals that 85% of people report struggling with self-confidence issues at some point in their lives.[1] We all know that self-confidence is a plus in our business, yet almost all of us struggle to achieve it.

Eighteen months ago, I changed my title in my Instagram bio to 'The UK's leading wedding industry marketing expert' and I felt a little bit sick about it. Who am I to proclaim to be the expert in my field? Surely people will scoff and laugh about my arrogance? I had been at a business conference for my own

---

1   Jannik Lindner, 'Gitnux Report 2024: New Self Confidence Statistics Reveal Impact on Success and Health', Gitnux, July 2024. Available at: https://gitnux.org/self-confidence-statistics.

self-development and the peers on my table had told me to lean into my expertise and shout about it – because, after all, if I don't shout about it, who will?

When they suggested the change to my bio, I laughed nervously and said, 'I can't do that.' 'OK,' they said, 'tell us who in the UK is better at wedding industry marketing than you?' I didn't have an answer. Then they asked, 'How many wedding businesses have you taught marketing to who have gone on to have huge business transformations and success?' 'Lots,' I said. Finally, they asked me to look back at my reviews and soak in all of the amazing comments people had written over the years about how my knowledge and teaching had helped them. There was a moment of silence before one of them said, 'See, you are the best at what you do. So, stop pretending you're not.'

Despite all of this, I still felt sick about actually writing it on paper. The fear of what other people would think was overwhelming. I remember telling this story to my Wedding Pro Members Lounge in the days after the event, and all of them telling me that I absolutely was the best, so of course I could say it.

That bio change has been one of the best things I have done in my business. Stepping into that place of confidence has given me more incredible opportunities to help wedding pros and wedding venues grow. Whenever I walk onto a stage now, guess how the host introduces me... 'Next up we have Becca Pountney – the UK's leading wedding industry marketing expert.'

## Finding your inner confidence?

Now that you have heard my struggle, I want you to consider your own introduction and how you can add a confidence twist to it.

Write a list of all of the things that you or your venue are amazing at, how you help couples, what makes you better than your competitors and also what other people have said about you in reviews. This will feel uncomfortable, because it's much easier to dwell on our insecurities – but stick with it and get as many things on paper as possible.

Once you have your list, look through it and work out if there are achievements or phrases that you could use in your own Instagram bio or on your website. Get used to talking about these things and believing them yourself. I know you are incredible at what you do, but do you know it yourself?

## What if you don't have much experience?

First of all, whenever someone says to me they don't have much experience in weddings, I stop them and remind them that every wedding venue and wedding business owner has to have a day one and that it's nothing to be ashamed of. Just because it's your day one, doesn't mean that you are not good at what you do! Experience is wider than just your wedding industry experience, so look back further.

I have had some incredible conversations on my podcast when I spoke to people about what they did 'before weddings', and quite often they have learnt huge amounts from their own unique experiences.

Mike the Wedding DJ cut his teeth on a Disney Cruise – wow. Hannah the Wedding Planner had been planning corporate and wedding events in a venue for years before her self-employed day one. Sam the photographer trained and worked as a nurse in the NHS before leaving her nursing career behind for wedding photography. Just look at my own journey, most of my marketing expertise came from working in the television and radio world, before I ever set foot into the wedding industry.

Your experience is unique to you. You will have had unique work and life experiences that give you a perspective unlike anyone else who's doing the same. So, lean into that and use it to your advantage. Taking the step to become self-employed is *huge*, so there will be something deep within you that said you had the skills, experience and ability. Now you need to bring that to the surface.

For those of you who are lacking in confidence, there are five common mistakes I see in the wedding industry. I want to address them all to save you from falling into the same traps. They feel like a good idea at the time but, after a while, you will see they were not such a good idea after all and they may actually do more harm than good to your wedding business growth.

If you have been in business for a few years already, you may find you have fallen into these traps already.

If this is you, remember none of us is perfect – so don't spend time dwelling on the past. It's time to move forward.

## Mistake 1: Working for free

I see countless posts in Facebook groups where 'new pros' offer their services for free to a wedding couple in order to build up a portfolio. Although people may jump at the offer, they are unlikely to be your 'ideal customers' for your portfolio.

The reality is that working a wedding is hard work. You need income to cover the cost of running a business and there's absolutely *no* need to give everything away for free. Not only are you putting a flashing light on your head and shouting to the world, 'I'm new and don't know what I'm doing' (which isn't great marketing), you are also feeding your own self-confidence doubts.

### THE ALTERNATIVE?

It's a good idea to get some experience under your belt of real wedding situations, and there are plenty of opportunities to get paid work as an assistant on a wedding day. Photographers will often look for 'second shooters', planners hire on-the-day assistants and DJs are often looking for a number two that can go on jobs for them.

Why not reach out to some local venues or catering teams to see if they need any extra temp staff during their busy times? These are all ways of building wedding day experience while being compensated for your time.

## NEED TO BUILD A PORTFOLIO?

Building a portfolio is the number 1 explanation people give when they have been doing weddings for free. I understand where you are coming from – a portfolio is important. However, there are other ways to build one.

Instead of giving away your time to a wedding that you have no control over, use the same time to arrange your own portfolio shoot. This way you can decide on the look and feel of the images, as well as ensuring you get all the shots you need. There are lots of other wedding pros who love to work on these shoots, just make sure you find people who have the same brand feel as you and that you have similar objections.

## THE EXCEPTION

There are times when you may offer your work for free – but this needs to be the exception and not the rule. When you consider these opportunities, you always need to weigh up the direct benefits of the opportunity to your business against your time. For example, a one-off trip to photograph a wedding venue for free in return for a place on their recommended supplier list could be a fair swap.

## Mistake 2: Perfectionism

You'll be familiar by now with my 'Done is better than perfect' mantra. I see perfectionism as a huge barrier to success for creatives, because nothing is ever quite ready for launch. It's very rare that anything is perfect first time. But it can always be improved and evolve. You don't need everything perfect before you launch into the world with your business. You just need the foundations in place and the confidence to put yourself out there.

We all struggle with perfectionism and procrastination from time to time. When I decided to launch a podcast, it took me a full year to get it off the ground, because I was scared of it not being good enough. Yet once it launched, it was amazing for my business. I wish I hadn't wasted that year worrying.

What's stopping you attracting clients? Why won't you hit 'Publish' on your website? Can you get it to a place where it's done… and then start to level it up to make it increasingly perfect?

I have learnt in my own business that the way to overcome my own perfectionist barriers is to tell people I am going to do something before I actually have everything in place – because that gives me a deadline and I have to deliver. For me, the worry of letting people down is much bigger than my fear of perfectionism.

## LEARN TO ACCEPT PRAISE

The next time someone sees your work and makes a comment about how amazing it is, just pause and say thank you. As a perfectionist, it's very easy to ignore their compliments and start pointing out the flaws and imperfections in your product, things that they hadn't even noticed. Instead, just soak it in and say thank you – and remember that piece of praise as a confidence-builder for the next time you doubt your own work and ability.

# Mistake 3: Trying to be the cheapest

I love the saying, 'The cheapest is never the best and the best is never the cheapest.' It's very difficult for a brand to be known as both best and cheapest. Yet the biggest mistake I see pros making as a direct result of their own lack of confidence is trying to undercut all of their competitors.

How did you come up with the pricing in your business? The majority of people I speak to said that they first looked at their peers and tried to undercut them as they thought that being cheaper would lead to more bookings.

A few years back, I ran an experiment on social media to prove that this method isn't effective. Why? Well, because there's someone else who's always willing to be cheaper than you.

I went into a Facebook group and pretended to be a bride. I asked if anyone would be willing to photograph my wedding for less than £500. If we bear in mind that almost every successful wedding photographer I know charges £1,000+ for their services, this felt like a huge ask. Imagine my surprise when I had at least twenty photographers reach out to me to say they would do it for the price I had asked.

With this knowledge, I went back again. However, this time I asked if anyone would be willing to photograph my wedding for free. This time I was even more shocked at the replies I got, practically begging me to allow them to my wedding.

This was a basic experiment. It certainly wasn't scientific and I couldn't tell you the quality or experience of the photographers that offered their services. However, it did prove the point I had been sharing with my clients. There is absolutely no point being the 'cheapest' as there will *always* be someone willing to do it for less than you, even for free.

The other problem with trying to be the cheapest is that it can set future customers' expectations too low and make it really hard for you to ever make a profit. I've had this conversation multiple times:

**Me:** Why are you launching at such a low cost?

**Wedding Pro:** I'm going to sell the first two at just £1,000 to get experience and then double my price.

**Me:** What about when the couple start recommending you to their friends? Are they not going to query why the price instantly doubled? That couple will be raving to everyone about how cheap you are.

Do you want to be known as the cheap wedding pro?

This isn't a sustainable strategy. You need to work out your price based on your costs, your work and the market position combined. (We will look at pricing in more detail in chapter 8.)

It was the belief that cheap = more sales that led to my favourite phrase that I share with my clients: Disney never discount.

Here in the UK, we have a number of theme parks and attractions, but there's an unwritten rule – we *never* pay full price to go. The gate price may be £75, but we know that on almost every cereal packet or hand soap you can find a 50% discount coupon, so you know you only ever have to pay £35 to go. This hugely devalues the ticket price, because only a few unsuspecting tourists are ever really paying the full amount.

When it comes to a Disney World holiday, it's another story. You know that it's not possible to get coupons to discount your entry. If you want to go, you pay the full price and it's not cheap. However, every year, millions of people pay it because they know that it's absolutely worth paying full price for.

Stop trying to be the cheapest. Instead, aim to be the best.

*Disney never discount.*

## Mistake 4: Worrying about what everyone else thinks

One of the biggest breakthroughs with my own inner confidence came in the autumn of 2022. I was at a business conference listening to keynote speaker Carrie Wilkerson, when she said something that resonated so much I find myself constantly sharing it with others.

> Stop worrying about what *they* think of you… Who are these imaginary *they* anyway? Do they pay your bills or live in your household?

At this moment, I realised I let this imaginary 'they' hold me back frequently. We can spend hours thinking through every aspect of our business, especially how we present ourselves in public. Often, the one thing that stops us going ahead is the worry about what 'they might think'.

From one florist who didn't want people to know her age in case they felt she was too young, to another florist who was worried clients would think she was too old, we all tend to worry about what other people may think. The reality is that both of these florists are incredible at what they do, their work speaks for itself and their age isn't a factor at all.

What if *they* think differently to you?

When I first started running Wedding Business Networking events, live video was a relatively new feature for Facebook and something I knew I should get on board with – but the idea of it was scary! What would I say, what would people think, would I make myself look silly or maybe my hair would be out of place? I very nearly talked myself out of the idea.

However, I pushed past my inner thoughts and recorded the video. I sat down on my bedroom floor (as it was the only plain background I had in my house at the time) and spoke to the camera all about my upcoming event. I explained who I was, how the event would work and I talked through every element so that, if you were on the fence about coming along, you wouldn't need to worry. From what to wear to how to make the most out of the evening, I covered it all. Once I had published the video, I wanted the ground to swallow me up. It was *so* embarrassing. What on earth would *they* all think?

On the night of the event, a lovely lady came over to me, introduced herself and thanked me for the video I had recorded. She explained that she was nervous about coming along but having watched the video, she felt a lot more confident and had had an amazing evening making lots of new connections.

At that moment, I realised it wasn't about me. People were not watching what I did in order to criticise my clothes, my hair or even how I spoke. They needed reassurance – and I could give them that. In fact, if I hadn't made that video, they might not have come at all.

We can't control what people think about us. But I think it's fair to say that most of the time we are all so wrapped up in our own lives that we are not that invested in judging everything around us. I think of all the videos and photos I see of clients online. I'm never thinking anything other than, 'Ooh, this sounds interesting.'

My advice to you is stay in your own lane and within your own moral compass. If you are happy with what you are saying and doing and you are being authentic, honest and

*Stop letting this imaginary 'they' hold you back.*

unapologetically you, then stop letting this imaginary 'they' hold you back. After all, you might be doing others a disservice by not putting your thoughts and knowledge confidently out into the world.

## Mistake 5: Comparing yourself with others

In the late 1800s, the then US president Theodore Roosevelt said that 'Comparison is the thief of joy' and I tend to agree with him.

In the wedding industry, almost every client I work with confesses that they struggle not to compare themselves to their peers. They also admit that comparisons do nothing for their self-confidence. Social media makes it *so* easy for us to look at all of the 'competitors' in our area and see what they are up to. Facebook groups and networking meetings can sometimes feel full of people who are hitting all their goals, leaving us feeling inadequate. Perhaps you have turned up to exhibit at a wedding showcase, only to find someone selling the same services with an exhibition stand that looks ten times better than what you have planned.

I find that some clients have spent hours dissecting their competitors' websites. They know their prices inside out and even know where they go on holiday. While they try and convince me it's all good market research, quite often it's a form of self-sabotage as we walk away feeling like other people have it all together and we don't.

## YOU ARE ON YOUR OWN UNIQUE JOURNEY

Quite often I'm asked how I found success so quickly. I have to be quick to point out it hasn't been quick at all – they just haven't seen the whole journey. People may see me on stage at big conferences or travelling the world to work and think *wow!* But they didn't see the years of hard work, creating videos on my bedroom floor and sending private messages to people asking if they wanted to come along to my small local networking nights. Overnight success stories are very rare – and often we don't see the full picture. If a brand-new speaker looked at my Instagram, they might feel like I had it all – but they are comparing themselves to a person eight years into a business journey.

My son loves music. He is ten and plays the guitar, drums and piano and has a good musical ear. If he compared himself to Phil Collins or Elton John, he would be left feeling pretty inadequate. They are, of course, streets ahead of him in terms of skill and have many years on him age-wise. If he looked to them as a direct comparison, he would give up! But when he has the opportunity to play one of his instruments in front of his peers, they are astounded. Most of them can't read any musical notes, let alone play three instruments.

There is no point wasting our energy on comparison, because there are so many nuances. No one else is at the same point as we are. We may look to others and be inspired, but if looking at others is causing us to doubt our own ability, it's not worth it. Run your own race and keep looking forward.

At Sports Day, I often spot children making the same mistake. They start the 100-metre race strong. They are winning. But then something tells them to look left and right to see where the other competitors are. It almost always results in them missing out on first place. They should have focused on their own race, yet instead they got distracted by what the others were doing.

When it comes to comparison, the only person you should compare yourself to is you! Are you further ahead than you were this time last year? Have you made more profit or built new connections? Have you hit the targets you set for yourself?

I love interviewing clients on my podcast about their journeys because they often leave the interview beaming! 'Wow, I had never reflected on just how much I have achieved,' they say. 'I feel so proud.'

Take time to reflect on your own journey, note it down or keep a diary of successes that you can read at the end of the year.

## EVERYONE IS AIMING AT A DIFFERENT TARGET

The other reason comparing ourselves is not beneficial is because we are often aiming for different targets. What we count as a win may be nothing to someone else.

A few months back, I came across a piece of paper in my seven-year-old daughter's drawer which she had entitled, 'This year's happy things'. I smiled as I glanced down the page and saw she had made notes of the trips we had taken and the day the tooth fairy came… and then I saw Number 5 – 'my verruca fell off'. I smiled to myself, took a quick photo (surely a great memory for a future wedding speech) and I popped it back into her drawer.

Later that evening, I confessed to her that I had found it and asked how something as basic (and slightly disgusting) had made the list alongside hotel visits and birthday parties. 'It may not be exciting to you, Mummy,' she whispered, 'but I've been waiting for that verruca to go for *ages* so I'm *very* happy about it.' Of course it made the list.

Your goal might be five weddings a year – perhaps someone else's is five hundred. You may want to work all hours of the day and travel the world. Someone else may just want enough to keep them occupied during the school day while they don't have 'parenting duties'. When you stop comparing and start putting that time and energy into your own goals and plans, you will achieve so much more.

## SOCIAL MEDIA IS NOT REALITY

Whenever you are social media scrolling, you have to keep in mind that it only tells you one part of the story. I have posted smiling pictures of me looking glam and sipping coffee, while in reality I've been at home, upset after finishing a counselling session. Social media as a business owner is marketing – it's not someone's whole life, it's a *piece* of their life that promotes their products and services. McDonald's doesn't advertise its burgers with a picture of a burger someone just ordered looking all flat and sloppy – their burgers all look juicy, with melting cheese oozing out. In the same way, business owners share the professional side of their business, their Insta-ready moments.

It may look like I am constantly working and never with my family, but that's because I'm not sharing the photos of me sitting at the side of the pool during a swimming lesson or at the football pitch, because that's personal. If you knew me, you would know that family is a huge part of my week. When you compare yourself to the tip of the iceberg, you don't really know what's going on beneath. So don't compare.

## Let's get practical

As we bring this chapter to a close, there may have been elements that have resonated with you, so I wanted to give you some practical ideas to help you move forward.

1.   Speak about it. If you're feeling underconfident, speak about it, especially to your peers because they are probably struggling with the same things. Be vulnerable and share how you are feeling. It will surprise you how many people are feeling the same way.

2.   Use the 'hide' feature on social media. If there are certain accounts that bring out negative feelings or make you feel bad about yourself, use the features on social media to help you. You can still remain connected to a contact but choose to 'hide posts' from them. This means they won't keep popping up in your feed and you can avoid looking at what they are doing all of the time.

3.   Keep a diary and set goals. This is the best way to see your own personal progress and to remind yourself of your own journey. Each small step along the road will get you closer to your bigger goals. 2016 Becca is very different to 2024 Becca – but I wouldn't have got to today without all those small steps along the way. You don't have to create a detailed business plan and marketing strategy for the next five years, just take a couple of steps. What are they going to be?

4.   Keep reading this book and do the work. Knowledge is power and, as you work your way through the chapters, I am going to be giving you advice and

guidance to help you along your journey. I'll help you get to grips with your numbers so you can be confident in your pricing and I'll give you guidance as you work towards your own personal goals.

# YOUR OFFER

Build your brand

What's your favourite brand? I often start my workshops by asking this question because everyone has a different answer. Whether you love Apple, Disney, Starbucks, Ralph Lauren or Primark, brands play a big part in our lives. According to a 2013 study by McAlister and Cornwell, children as young as three recognise brand logos and start to form an opinion.[1] As a parent myself, I know my children have been able to spot famous toy stores and fast-food restaurants for years, usually followed by incessant begging to pay them a visit.

When we start our own wedding businesses, we don't tend to put our businesses in the same category as these bigger brands, mainly because we don't have the same multi-million-pound advertising budgets as they do. However, there is a huge amount we can learn from these big players that we can use in our own businesses.

## Your own brand loyalty

What are some of your favourite brands? Perhaps clothing retailers you regularly use or the car you drive. What is it about that brand that you like? Think about the logos they choose, their brand colours, the way they advertise, and how that brand makes you feel. These are not accidental choices. Companies spend huge amounts of time and money to ensure they evoke particular

---

1   Anna R. McAlister and T. Bettina Cornwell, 'Children's brand symbolism understanding: Links to theory of mind and executive functioning', *Psychology & Marketing* 27, no. 3 (2010): 203–28. https://doi.org/10.1002/mar.20328.

thoughts and feelings in you, to keep you spending money with them.

One of my favourite brands is Tiffany. I love the elegance of the products, the signature Tiffany Blue and the way I feel when I walk into one of their shops. When I turned eighteen, my parents bought me a Tiffany bracelet. Tiffany had always been such an aspirational brand for me and I still have that bracelet safely stored in my Tiffany pouch.

When you study your favourite brands carefully, you will start to see all of the little touches that contribute to why you are drawn to them – from the consistent colours they use and the fonts they choose to how the store smells and the way they package their products and services. There is a lot we can learn from the biggest players in the market.

## Who are you for?

In order to establish your brand, you need to spend some time thinking through who you are for. 'Everyone' isn't an answer. When we build a business aimed at everyone, we end up attracting nobody. Chanel is not targeting the same people as H&M. Neither is right or wrong, they are just different.

I'm going to ask you a series of questions to help you understand who your brand is for. Take some time to think these through and make some notes. If you are struggling, think about one of your past clients that you loved working with, or base it on friends you have that you would love to have worked for. There are no right or wrong answers, but the clearer you can be on who you are for, the better. We are creating a dream client – the client that, if they came to you, you would *love* to work at their wedding.

1.  How old are your couple and what jobs do they have?

2.  Where are they living? Are they getting married where they live or elsewhere?

3.  What's important to your couple? What are their core values for their wedding?

4.  What is their budget?

5.  What other suppliers have they booked for their day?

6.  What three venues did they tour and which one have they booked?

7.  Do they have children?

8.  What kind of meal are they having?

9.  How many guests are at the wedding?

10. What three words would you use to describe the vibe of the wedding day?

11.  What would they hate to have at their wedding?

12.  Why did they want to book you?

Once you have worked through these questions, you should be able to describe your dream couple clearly in a couple of sentences. You can even give them names if you like.

Here's an example: imagine for a moment I'm a florist.

My dream couple are Courtney and Ben. They are a down-to-earth couple with corporate jobs in London, but they want to get married out in the countryside where they grew up. They have a high budget but they want the overall vibe to be laid-back luxury. Family is hugely important, so the guest list will be large and full of children. Sustainability is a big factor in their planning process, so they are making sure each of their suppliers has a similar ethos. They want to spend money on big floral arrangements to impress their friends and to ensure the photos look incredible.

*You should be able to describe your dream couple clearly in a couple of sentences.*

You should be able to introduce your couple to me as if they are your friends. Can you picture them and their wedding day?

Now you have your target couple identified, you need to keep them front and centre of your mind as you start to make branding and marketing decisions. Are the images you are sharing likely to appeal to Courtney and Ben? Does your brand resonate with them?

When I worked in radio, we had our 'ideal radio listeners' profiles up on a huge board in the meeting room. We had photos and a short bio about each one of the three ideal listeners. Whenever we came up with a competition or marketing idea in a meeting, we would glance at the board and ask each other, 'Would they be interested?' You may not have a meeting room with a large noticeboard, but the principle is the same. Now, whenever you make decisions, you need to ask yourself, 'Would my couple be interested? Or am I going in the wrong direction?'

## Your brand guide

Your business should have a basic set of brand guidelines that are available for you to access whenever you need them. If you have paid a brand designer to create your brand for you, this will have likely been given to you as part of their service, but if you have started from scratch you will need to produce this yourself.

A brand guide ensures you are consistent and it will help you communicate your values and unique offer effectively. It is a way of ensuring that every part of your business from the website to a printed banner or business card are consistent. If you take on a team member or hire a freelance team, having your brand guide in one place that you can share with them is important. In this next section, I am going to break down the different areas of your brand guide to ensure you have everything covered.

## 1. Colours

Not all colours are created equal, as two of my clients discovered when they planned a styled shoot a couple of years ago. The agreed theme of the shoot was 'blue', a seemingly easy brief, yet what actually happened was a disaster. When the different shoot suppliers started turning up with their 'blue' objects, it became clear very fast that everyone had a wildly different interpretation of what blue actually meant. The photoshoot ended up with a mishmash of unmatching items, and the result was a waste of everyone's time.

Every colour has a variety of shades, just spend a moment in the 'white section' of a paint store and you will see exactly what I mean. The iconic Virgin Atlantic red is subtly different from the Coca-Cola red and never will the two interchange. The branding teams know exactly what shade they use and everything will be reproduced in the correct colour.

### LET'S FIND YOUR BRAND COLOURS

In order to have the same brand consistency, you need to identify the key colours that you want to use in your brand and find out the 'hex number' or 'RGB number' for your colour.

In my business, I have an iconic Becca blue. I even have my office wall painted in this exact shade so that you see it whenever I go live. Becca blue has the Hex Code 91D6DF, so whenever I create something on Canva or have something printed, I give them the colour code to ensure it matches.

*A brand guide ensures you are consistent and will help you communicate your values and unique offer effectively.*

If you are starting from scratch or want to go through a mini rebrand, then websites like www.rgbcolorcode.com are a great starting place. You can look through the colours, decide on the ones you want to use and make a note of the codes underneath. It will give you the information that you need. I recommend having a main colour – just like my Becca blue or the Coca-Cola red – and then accent colours to go alongside it.

If you had a brand designer work on your website or logo, go back and ask them if they can send you your 'hex codes' and 'RGB colours'. They should have them noted down somewhere.

If you have created everything yourself, it's time to do some detective work. Even if you have been guessing your colour shades up to this point, from today we can start fresh and ensure you always keep your colours consistent. There are websites that will allow you to upload an image and then identify the colours it thinks are in the image. Upload your logo onto the site and see what colours it picks out. It may not be an exact science, but it will give you a starting point.

## USE YOUR COLOURS CONSISTENTLY

Now you have your colours selected, ensure they are added to a brand guide and in a place where you can access them easily. If you use Canva, you can 'add a brand kit' which will allow you to save your colours and use them in every design moving forward. Start using hints of the colour everywhere from social media to clothing in a brand shoot – and just like recognising Becca blue, people will start to identify that colour to you and your business.

## 2. Fonts

Choosing the right fonts to use in your business can influence how a potential customer reads your message. A good font needs to be easy to read, stand out on a page or screen and represent your brand identity.

Recently, I drove through one of the local villages and noticed a new restaurant was opening. The sign had been put up outside. As I drove past, I tried to read the sign but the font was very small and in a calligraphy style and I couldn't decipher the name of the business. I wanted to go home and look the business up, to discover the cuisine they were offering and when they were planning to open.

But the font on the sign meant I was no clearer about any of these answers.

We don't often notice font choices until something doesn't quite work. Imagine being sent a contract for a business that was all written in Comic Sans. You wouldn't take it seriously.

I recently received an email home from school where the teacher had accidentally written the whole email in a script text that looked like something from the 1900s and it was the talk of the playground. The message of the email was lost because the strange, out-of-place font had taken all the attention.

Go back to some of your favourite brands and see if you can identify their fonts, or ones that are similar. As with colours, there are websites that will identify fonts from an image and others that categorise fonts by similarity. You can use Canva as well.

When choosing your fonts, I recommend using a maximum of three different choices that work well together. Perhaps one font is always used for your headlines and you have an alternative font for larger paragraphs of text on your website. Make sure that one of the fonts that you choose is available in Microsoft Word, or whatever programme you use for letters, contracts, etc. Whatever you choose, get the names of the fonts added to your brand guidelines, and any notes about where they should or shouldn't be used. For example, I have a script font that looks really pretty, but I only use it to highlight the occasional word on social media or on my website – it would never work if I wrote a whole paragraph in it.

## 3. Logos

Creating a logo for your business will help set the tone for your business as it will be used throughout your marketing to tie your brand together. I recommend getting help from a professional brand designer to create your initial logo although you could create your own using Canva. A professional logo designer will spend time understanding your business as a whole – who you want to attract and how you want the logo to be used.

When you create a logo, I recommend creating several versions that can be used across different places. For example, a logo may need to be on a white or transparent background; it may need to fit in a circle or a square. You can even select elements of your logo to use as a brand mark. I use my full Becca Pountney logo on documents but I also regularly use my BP brand mark on social media. I even have a jumper with it on!

## 4. Tone of voice

The final section of your brand guidelines needs to cover your tone of voice. Do you speak in the first or third person? For example, do you say, 'I love working on vegan wedding cakes' or do you prefer to say, 'At Becca's cake company, we love to work on vegan wedding cakes'?

What is your writing style? Do you write in a serious or classic tone? Are you trying to be approachable, laid back, funny – or, like me, overly enthusiastic! I recently asked AI to decipher my tone of voice from my own copy and it said this:

> Becca writes in a relatable and motivational style, using personal anecdotes and a conversational approach to guide and inspire creative professionals in building successful wedding businesses. Becca's tone is encouraging and understanding, conveying a sense of empathy for the doubts and insecurities faced by individuals navigating the business aspects of their creative endeavors.

I thought this description was incredibly accurate. I like to use positive, uplifting language with plenty of emojis and far too many explanation marks. I try to write how I speak, so hopefully if you are reading this on paper you can imagine it being read in my voice.

If I was to employ a copywriter or social media manager, I would want them to have a copy of my 'tone of voice' guidelines so that they could closely match the style, to sound like me. A good brand will have a clear and consistent tone of voice.

Once you have written your 'tone of voice' description down, get it added to your brand guidelines along with your colours and fonts. You now have a clear document to work from whenever you create something new for your business.

Now you have the look of your brand, it's time to consider some of the other areas that make your brand consistent. It's easy to think that your brand is just a logo, but the most successful brands combine multiple elements to help them become recognisable.

## 5. Appealing to the senses

When working on physical spaces, shops will spend time thinking about how each aspect of the brand will appeal to your five senses. As humans we respond to each of the senses, but have you ever considered how you could use them in your business?

*Sight:* When you walk into a designer brand store, you know immediately that it's expensive. The way the items are displayed, the lighting in the store, the immaculate looking staff and the bouncer on the door. Every part of this experience screams luxury at you.

Have you considered how you dress for a client meeting and how that could impact their view of your brand? Where do you meet your clients? If it's in person, are you meeting them in a place that matches your brand identity? If you are presenting as high end, a meeting at your local fast-food restaurant wouldn't be a good brand match. When they see your work online, do customers know immediately what your brand stands for from the images?

*Sound:* Do you ever stop to notice the music choices playing when you walk into a shop? These carefully curated playlists don't just happen by accident, they are there for a reason. I listened to an interview with the entrepreneur Stephen Bartlett about how he prepares his podcast guests before he interviews them. Before they arrive, he researches what their favourite music is and arranges to have it playing in the waiting room before the interview. He doesn't tell them he does this, it's just a subtle touch that he knows will help them relax and put them in a good mood ahead of the interview.

A bridal store owner I spoke with recently explained that she has a list of songs that her customers plan to walk down the aisle to which she plays them while her brides try on dresses. It helps to put them into that 'bridal' mood without them realising.

You may not have a physical store, but are you thinking through the music choices on your Instagram reels or TikTok videos, and considering if they are on brand? Are you ensuring you meet with your clients to talk about their wedding in a quiet space, rather than somewhere bustling with people?

Sound is not the first thing we may think of when it comes to branding, but it is one worth paying attention to.

*Touch:* One of the things I miss about shopping online is being able to touch the items before I purchase them. There's something about being able to feel a piece of fabric or the shape of something that helps with the buying process. At first glance, it may seem impossible to have 'touch' as part of your brand. However, there are a few ways you could incorporate elements of it.

If you have a physical meeting space or store, then adding in cushions or soft rugs can help a space feel more relaxing. Wedding photographers can bind their albums in luxurious materials. Having one to share with couples during a consultation gives them the chance to 'touch' your work. Perhaps you don't meet your couple until the wedding day or just before. In this case, why not send them a postcard or handwritten note as part of your on-boarding process. That way, not only do they feel special and thankful that they booked you, but you have also added in an element of touch into your brand.

*Taste:* If you are a cake maker or work with food in some capacity, you can tick this box right away. You should always have samples of your work to share at wedding shows, client meetings and venue visits. When I used to exhibit at wedding shows with my wedding videography business, I noticed that the biggest crowds were often seen at the wedding cake tables. This was no coincidence. The guests were on the lookout for free cake. I quickly realised that having some sweets on my table helped to start a conversation.

At a venue training day that I ran recently, the venue team served waffles during the coffee break. Not only was this a delicious, unexpected treat, it also became one of the most talked about parts of the day. Taste is memorable.

How could you add in a memorable 'taste' element to your brand? I know some wedding pros who send tea bags as part of their on-boarding gift and suggest that the couple drink the tea while looking through all of the information. Perhaps when you meet clients, you always hand out 'love hearts' or offer a mint at the start of a meeting. When I signed up to work with my current web designer Becky Lord, she sent me an amazing welcome pack. One of the items enclosed was Prosecco Fluff – a kind of candy floss that you could pop on the top of your glass – which tasted incredible! Not only was this unique, but I also still talk about it with friends three years later and it always reminds me of Becky and her business.

*Smell:* Have you ever walked into the clothing store Hollister? The moment you step through the door, the scent hits you. They must spray it everywhere. What about the soap store Lush? You can smell that shop even before you have entered it. I usually give it a miss because it's just too much for my senses. There are not many brands that you can identify by scent alone, but there are some. Your sense of smell is connected to your memory and a single scent can transport you back to a moment in time, almost instantly.

Disneyworld uses subtle scents pumped out into their parks to encourage their customers to feel certain emotions or to incentivise them to buy. As you walk down Main Street, the smell of candy is pumped out onto the streets. Just look along the bottom of some of the shop windows and you will see the vents. The various smells at Disneyworld have become so iconic you can even purchase the candles to match various rides-attraction smells, so you can have that memory even when you return home. Disney understands the power of scents – that's why they spend so much money on them.

If you own a physical store or venue, then finding a signature fragrance is a good idea. Spend some time researching the different emotions a scent evokes and then find a good match and use it consistently. If a customer visits multiple times, they will subliminally start to match that scent with your business. When you are attending a wedding or client meeting, you too could have a signature scent that you spray just before you walk in. We have all shaken hands with someone whose perfume or aftershave smells divine! Sometimes before I send a postcard or gift to a client, I will spray my perfume over it, so that it has a subtle sweet smell when it arrives at the other end. Next time you receive something from me in the post, give it a sniff and see if the scent remains.

## 6. Your business associations

As you will discover in later chapters, I am a big believer in building industry connections to build your brand. I will encourage you to make connections with absolutely everyone. However, you do need to be more selective if they start to become part of your marketing, because when you recommend another business to your clients, you need to make sure that their brand values and ideal couple are in alignment with yours. If you are working on a photoshoot, ensure that all of the elements of the shoot come from suppliers with a similar look and ethos, otherwise it will look mismatched. When choosing which venues to promote online or which wedding fairs to attend, first do your research and check that your 'ideal clients' are likely to be there. When a high-end florist exhibits at a low-end hotel, they look out of place and are unlikely to book any work. When a photographer who specialises in grand mansion house weddings exhibits in a barn, it becomes confusing to clients. Remember that the other businesses that you associate with publicly will have an impact on your brand.

Whenever I work with a brand or invite a guest on my podcast, I take the responsibility very seriously. I know if I introduce someone to you publicly that you will also associate them with me. I have a set of core business values and I want to ensure the guests I work with align with them, otherwise it would be a mismatch. I don't always get it right. I once had to issue an apology to my clients about a business association which wasn't a good fit. I've also spoken at events where the person on stage after me contradicts everything that I would teach. Sometimes that's unavoidable. However, where possible I bring you the best people and I hope your desire is to do the same for your couples.

## 7. Your personality

For almost all of you, you are the central cog in your brand's wheel. It's you that the couples meet with, you are there on the wedding day, and when they are buying your business they are buying you. Even if you work as part of a bigger team such as a venue, it's you that they are dealing with regularly.

I once went to an event by business coach and founder of 'Youpreneur', Chris Ducker. He asked us which parts of our personality our clients would identify us by. He explained that his personality elements were 'being British', 'Whisky' and 'Bonsai Trees'. These were all things that were at the core of his identity, but he emphasised and talked about them as part of his business more than anything else. I hadn't really noticed this before, but as he explained it, I realised I did associate all of these things with him. When I saw a 'Bonsai Tree' Lego set in a shop, it had made me think 'Chris would like this'.

In that moment, I decided to implement a similar brand strategy. My three core personality elements are Disney, musical theatre and the Spice Girls. These are all things I truly enjoy – I just talk about them more frequently now. In stage talks, I describe myself as a Wannabe Spice Girl and explain that my 'why' is to book more trips to Disneyworld. If we have an in-person event, I will always request a Spice Girls song, and even my 'goal setting planner' that you can purchase has a musical theatre theme. You may not have realised but subliminally some of you will have started linking these things with me and my brand. Whenever the Spice Girls make the news, or someone is going to a musical theatre show, I get DMs because it reminded them of me!

What elements of your personality could you bring to the front of your business? I have clients who love Harry

Potter, always drink tea, love cats or even make the most incredible-looking salads. When we talk about these things, they become part of our brand and give people an insight into who we are.

## 8. Your brand as a whole

Becca, do we really need to add all of these elements into our business? This feels like a lot of work, I hear you cry. Although you don't need every single one of these elements immediately, I want to open your mind to the idea that a brand is more than just your logo or a few colours on a piece of paper. If you want to build a successful brand, you need to look at how all of the elements fit together to make you memorable, and then implement the ones that work best for you.

## Let's get practical

Now I have shared the theory, it's time to action some of this learning into your own business. Don't be a perfectionist. Just get started!

1.  Choose a brand that you love, and do some deep-dive thinking on how they showcase their brand. Look at the way they advertise, their choice of colours and fonts and how they present their brand messages to you. We can learn a lot by looking at the most successful brands.

2.  Work through the questions and identify your 'ideal couple'. Having this clear in your mind will help you make branding and marketing decisions down the line.

3.  Create your brand guide document: list the key elements of your brand including your logo, colours, fonts and tone of voice. Add in any new elements that you want to use consistently – from scents to sounds, personality traits and the peers you want to associate with. You will find lots of brand guide templates online to get you started.

# MARKETING

Start the puzzle

I love a jigsaw puzzle, especially a Disney-themed one. There's something relaxing about sitting and sorting through all of the tiny pieces to select the right one, and something very satisfying about completing that last piece and standing back to admire the finished result.

Working out how to market your business can feel like the moment you sit down to start your puzzle. There are so many pieces to choose from and it can feel overwhelming just thinking about where to start. Not only do you need to make the right choices, but they also need to seamlessly fit together to create the beautiful picture. In this chapter, I want to guide you through the world of marketing your wedding business, one small step at a time. I want to show you what's possible so that you can choose which piece to start with and work out how to ensure they all slot together. This is by no means an exhaustive list of options, but it will give you the foundations to start putting your wedding business out into the world.

## What is marketing?

In its simplest form, marketing is just telling people you exist and why they need to buy from you. In essence you could have the most incredible product in the world, but if you never tell anyone about it, you won't make any sales.

If you have ever seen the musical *Chicago*, you will know there is a character who sings a song called 'Mr Cellophane'. Amos Hart, the cast-off husband, sings a song about how other people look right through him, walk right past him and never even know he's there. Wedding business owners often fall into the category of Mr Cellophane because, despite being amazing at what you do, it feels like nobody knows you exist. I have met many a venue owner or wedding pro who feels like they have become the best-kept secret. They know they have great things to offer, but that message is struggling to get out. If this is how you feel, then it's a marketing problem that you have. In order to make sales, you need to get your message known by the right people, and we do that through marketing.

*When you think you are visible enough in your wedding business, remember that Coca-Cola are still advertising.*

Despite being one of the biggest and most recognisable drinks brands in the world, in 2022 Coca-Cola still spent over 4 billion US dollars in advertising. Coca-Cola knows that there are new people being born every day that don't yet know about their drink, so they keep on marketing themselves to ensure they stay on top of the game. As wedding businesses, we don't have Coca-Cola's marketing budget, but we can adopt the same ethos because there are new people getting engaged every single day that you need to talk to about your business. One of the challenges I often set out when I talk on stage is this: 'When you think you are visible enough in your wedding business, remember that Coca-Cola are still advertising.'

## Where to start?

There are two key factors to take into consideration when deciding where to spend your marketing time and money.

1.   Where are your ideal couple spending their time?

2.   Where do you feel most comfortable?

### 1. WHERE ARE YOUR COUPLES SPENDING THEIR TIME?

In the last chapter, I set you an exercise to work out who your ideal couple were and what defined them. Now you have that clear in your head, it's time to start thinking through where they spend their time and how they are doing their wedding planning. What platforms do they use online? What kind of venues are they looking at? Are they getting recommendations from a wedding planner or from their venue? Are they attending wedding fairs and if so which ones?

They key to successful marketing is ensuring you are meeting people where they are at. I once went to a horse show on an outing with my parents. As well as the racing, there were plenty of stands selling all kinds of items. Take, for example, the stand that was selling specialist horse saddles. They had quite a lot of interest and I'm sure they made a substantial number of sales. The reason for their success? They were marketing in the perfect place – to a huge crowd of people who were interested in horses. If that same stall had set up in the middle of a supermarket or at the local village fair, do you think they would have been so successful? The product and the price would have been exactly the same, but the location would have killed their sales.

I once spoke to a luxury wedding photographer who told me that being recommended by venues was a waste of time and that he never got any clients from them. When I dug a little deeper and found out the venues he was being recommended by, this was no surprise. If your target client is getting married in a high-cost mansion house in the countryside and you are being recommended in a city-centre chain hotel, there is a mismatch. You are being seen in the wrong place, by the wrong kinds of people.

To start to uncover the answer about where your couples are spending their time both online and in person, you need to do some market research. Do they have preferred social media platforms? Do they read articles from particular publications? Which wedding shows are they likely to be at?

Start asking people who fit into your ideal client type how they planned their wedding. If an ideal couple make an enquiry, chat with them over the phone and ask them about their wedding planning process. When speaking with directories or wedding shows, ask them about the demographics of their client base to check it's a good fit. Go to wedding open events where you think your ideal clients may be attending and get chatting with people. Find out their wedding planning process. Ask your fellow wedding pros. Find people who work with the type of client you are trying to attract and find out what works for them. How about putting yourself into the shoes of your ideal couple and seeing what you can find online? When it comes to marketing, there is not a one-size-fits-all answer to how you should do it. You need to find the solutions that work best for you.

## 2. WHERE DO YOU FEEL MOST COMFORTABLE?

The key to great marketing is consistency. You need to repeat a message multiple times and in multiple places for people to remember it. If you want to be consistent, then it's a great idea to start where you feel comfortable. That way, you are much more likely to succeed.

Do you love to write? Do you have beautiful imagery to share? Do you like live video? Do you prefer to be out in person meeting people face-to-face? Which platforms do you feel comfortable using and which ones do you understand? Do you want to do everything yourself, or have other people help you?

Write out a list of your skills and where you feel most comfortable. For example, if you are good at writing, then blog post creation or magazine article submissions could be a good place to start. If you are great on video content, then perhaps a video-heavy social media platform would work well for you. Perhaps you find it easier in person. If this is you, then attending multiple wedding shows, networking events and in-person venue meetings could be the way to go.

Now put your lists together. Cross reference the list of where your couples spend time and your list of skills and look for the cross over. When you find the marketing sources that are on both lists, these are where I would suggest you start. For example if you know your ideal couples spend time on video-led social media channels, and creating short-form video content is one of your strengths, this would be a great place for you to start.

## It's not about cost, it's about ROI

Stop making all your decisions based on how much something costs and, instead, start focusing on the ROI (return on investment). While some marketing strategies are expensive, they may quickly pay for themselves through the leads they generate. There are plenty of cost-free marketing sources – but they often require more time and effort to achieve similar results.

Think about a wedding directory, for example. It may be expensive, but it will expose your business to numerous potential clients. You may be able to get the same number of eyeballs through Google – but this will require both time and knowledge. Local marketing, like a £50 table at a hotel event, is cheap – but maybe only five couples show up. In contrast, a £1,500 stand at a national wedding exhibition could put you in front of 5,000 people.

*Start focusing on the return on investment.*

When spending money on marketing of any form, it's crucial that you work out the return on investment you need to make it a success. If you spend £1,000 on a piece of marketing, it needs to generate more than £1,000 in sales to be a success. You need to look at the numbers and the facts rather than gut instinct.

Although it's not always easy to discover exactly where couples come from, there are a few things you can implement to start to measure your ROI more accurately. Here are a few practical ideas:

1. Add a box to your website enquiry form asking how they found you.

2. On consultation calls, ensure that the question of how they found you is part of the conversation.

3. When an enquiry converts, make sure you note where that enquiry came from so that, at the end of the year, you can see which marketing sources were the most successful.

4. Regularly look at the 'Acquisition' section of your Google Analytics to see which sources are leading people to your website.

5.   When you collect email addresses, whether at events or through online offers, make sure to note in your email marketing system where each contact comes from using labels or tags. This way, if someone becomes a customer, you can easily see how they first connected with your business. It helps you understand which methods are working best to attract clients.

At the end of a year, I should be able to sit down and have a conversation with you about where you customers came from, what marketing had the best conversion rates and what the return on investment was for each thing you paid for. If you don't have these answers yet, then this is what you need to aim for if you want to ensure you make wise marketing decisions.

## Where can you market your wedding business?

Now I have shared some guidance on how to choose your marketing sources, I am going to share some of the most popular places to market your wedding business or venue. I will share the upsides and the downsides of each area as well as some best practice tips to get you started.

We are going to think about five different ways you can market your business:

1.   Social media

2.   Your website

3.  Wedding directories

4.  Wedding shows

5.  PR and media

## 1. Social media

✔ Pros:  It's free and pretty much anyone can work out how to use it.

✗ Cons:  You have no control over the algorithms and they could remove you from their platform at any moment.

This section focuses on best practices and overarching strategies for social media, rather than platform-specific details. Given the speed at which social media plat-forms and their user experiences change, concentrating on granular details would make this book out-of-date almost immediately. Instead, I will outline principles that you can apply to any social media platform.

### THE SHOP WINDOW

When I speak about social media platforms, I like to compare them with a shop window. When you are wandering down a high street full of shops, you tend to browse the shop windows until something entices you inside the shop. Your social platforms are your businesses equivalent of the shop window. Your potential customers are scrolling their phones until something entices them to stop. Your job is to get their attention.

Sales are rarely made in the shop window – they happen inside of the shop. Apply this same thought process to your social platforms. Although your social presence may entice them in, or even provoke an initial contact, most of the time the sale will happen on your website or on a call.

## YOUR BEST WORK SHOULD BE IN YOUR SHOP WINDOW

It's very rare that a shop puts their least popular or outdated items in the shop window. They are trying to draw your attention to their most popular looks, styled in a way to entice you inside. When you are considering what to post on your social media, you need to have this same ethos. You should be showcasing your best work, with professional images or video clips that showcase what you can do in the best possible light.

There are spaces where you can share more casual, behind-the-scenes aspects of your business, but the front and centre of your profile should be your best work. If I landed on your social page today, would the first thing I saw be truly reflective of your brand and something you would be proud of? If not, perhaps you need to make some changes.

## SHOW WHAT YOU WANT TO SELL, NOT WHAT YOU ARE SELLING

Social media can sometimes feel like a chicken-and-egg situation. You want to attract a higher-spending couple or a different type of style, yet all your images reflect something different. The truth is that you will sell what your customers see, because they assume that's what you do.

I had a cake maker once who wanted to move away from the rustic wedding cake in a barn to a more elegant, contemporary cake style. When I looked over her social media, every image she was showing was of a naked-style, rustic wedding cake, so it's no surprise every enquiry was asking for that exact style. In order to shift what you sell, you need to make the first move. In this example, creating a couple of dummy cakes in the new style and getting them professionally photographed would have allowed her to shift her brand presence and start attracting a new type of client. Your social media should paint a picture of where you are aspiring to be, rather than where you are right now. It's a marketing tool, not a record of completed work.

## SOCIAL MEDIA IS DESIGNED TO BE SOCIAL

Do you ever feel stuck with your social media presence? You just want to use it as a platform to sell your services, but no one is particularly interested? Does it feel like you are talking to thin air? If this resonates with you, then you probably need to go back to the origins of social media, rather than just continuing to post the same things.

In essence, social media was designed to be *social* – for friends to keep in touch, share images and keep connected. Although it continues to evolve, this is still the heart of why people are on the platforms. We don't go there to constantly be sold to.

Take a few minutes to note down the social media profiles that you love to follow. What makes you smile, what stops your scroll and what would make you save a post? I love to follow Disney vloggers. I love seeing all of their tips and tricks and I like to live vicariously through them as they holiday in Florida while I am sitting at home in rainy England. Perhaps you go to social media for cleaning hacks, recipe ideas, planning tips or clothing inspiration. Most users don't go to social media primarily for its adverts, so why do we tend to think of our business social media posts that way, as a constant advert?

What can you learn from the accounts you enjoy following and how can you bring some of those elements into what you do to promote your brand?

## WHAT SHOULD I POST ON SOCIAL MEDIA?

Have you ever sat in front of a screen and thought, I have no idea what to post on social media? If that's you, then these three content pillars are designed to help you keep your feed interesting to clients, while also ensuring you always have something to post.

- Education: We love to get tips and ideas and learn from social media, so why not use your social feeds to educate your potential clients? Most of them will never have planned a wedding before, so things that seem straightforward to you can be really helpful for them. Take some of your Frequently Asked Questions and turn them into posts.

- Entertainment: We love social content that makes us smile. This could be something funny, something emotive or even something interactive. Get engagement from your followers with polls or ask them for their opinions. Tell stories about your couples. Bring you and your team to the front of your profiles. We love to see real people doing day-to-day tasks, just look at the success of reality TV.

- Inspiration: Have you ever found yourself watching home renovation videos online and being amazed when you see the finished product? When couples are planning their wedding, they want to immerse themselves in the wedding world, and we can provide plenty of inspiration. Share your lavish set-ups, your stunning styled shoots and make your followers say, wow! Why not film or photograph a room before and after set-up so that you can show the transformation of the space? Your phone gallery is probably full to the brim with inspiration. It's time to share it with the world.

## CLEAR CALLS TO ACTION

As much as we want to engage our followers, a page full of pretty pictures will be unlikely to generate any sales. Although we don't want to constantly create ads, we do need to be giving our followers clear calls to action to encourage them to take the next steps. Encouraging them inside the shop by sending them to your website, encouraging them to send you a direct message or asking them to comment a key word under your post are all ways you can start a conversation and encourage them through the door.

## SIXTY POST IDEAS FOR YOU

A few years ago, I put together a resource which includes sixty social media post ideas for your wedding business. If you would like a copy, just scan the QR code below:

Despite taking a lot of time and effort, social media is still one of the most effective tools for reaching the right people fast. Used correctly, it can bring you new customers and eyes on your business for little to no cost

– something business owners could only have dreamt of twenty-five years ago. One of the biggest hurdles to creating social content is knowing what to post, so this resource should aid you in getting started.

## 2. Your website

✔ Pros:   A great website can sell your services and bring in new leads.

✘ Cons:   You need technical knowledge to keep it updated, or you will need to pay your web developer to make updates for you.

Now we have worked on your shop window, it's time to look at the shop itself – your website. In the 2024 Bridebook report couples were asked where they researched their wedding pros and venues.[1] Websites were in the top three, alongside Instagram and digital brochures. We know that couples are looking at your website before deciding whether or not to get in touch, so is it up to scratch?

### CLEAR AND CONCISE

When a client lands on your website, you have milliseconds to make a good impression – the first thing they see needs to make them stay. Your site needs to load fast or

---

1   The UK Wedding Report 2024, Bridebook, 2024, https://partners.bridebook.com/uk/uk-wedding-report-2024.

they will lose interest, so run regular website speed tests using one of the free online tools that are available.[2]

You also need to bear in mind the number of people that will visit your website using their phone or tablet. It's essential that you check that it's optimised for mobile.[3]

Once they have landed, they are looking for the information they need in a clear and concise fashion. Don't have too many options on the navigation bar – my recommendations are to keep it simple with:

- Services
- Investment
- About
- Portfolio
- Contact

You may have a blog or podcast or some other additional pages, but don't repeat the same information over various pages. We don't need your potential clients to get lost.

### PRICING

There are many debates about whether pricing should sit on your website – and I am a big believer that it should. Today's couples like transparency. They want to know what they are getting for their money, but that doesn't

---

2   pagespeed.web.dev
3   Laura Ceci, Mobile internet usage worldwide, 16 May 2024,
    https://www.statista.com/topics/779/mobile-internet.

mean they want cheap either. Ensuring your pricing is clear and easy to find will filter potential clients almost immediately. If they can't afford you, they won't get in touch. If they can afford you, they are part way to going ahead before they even get on a call.

The minimum I would want to see on your website is a 'From' price for each of your services, but the clearer you can be the better.

## CLEAR NEXT STEPS

Is it clear what the next steps are for your couple if they like what they see? I have been in plenty of shops where it's hard to find the checkout. Sometimes I just give up. We don't want our customers to abandon ship before they have made contact with us. Ensuring all paths lead to the same place, with a clear set of actions that your couple need to take to work with you, will reduce friction and also increase the likelihood of them enquiring.

## TESTIMONIALS

Gone are the days when testimonials are hidden on a page deep within your website. You want them to be front and centre. Testimonials are great social proof and show your future customers why they can trust you. Start sprinkling testimonials on every page of your website so they can't be missed.

## PODCAST

If this is something that appeals to you, podcasts can be really helpful in getting your name and services found in Google searches. They also give potential clients a glimpse of your personality and what you offer.

## GOOGLE SEARCHES

If you really want to be found by couples, then ensuring you turn up in Google searches is essential. I am amazed at how many of my clients neglect SEO (Search Engine Optimisation), even though it's one of the best places to collect new leads, for free. SEO is not my area of expertise, but you should be aiming to get to page 1 of Google for your keywords. Adding blog posts regularly to your website can be a great way to get found. I recommend adding a new post once a month and thinking through the keywords you want to be found for.

If SEO is on your to-do list, then I recommend you get further help. I have some great guest training inside of the Wedding Pro Members Lounge, so why not start there?

## 3. Wedding directories

✔ Pros:   They are doing the SEO and marketing work to help get your business in front of lots of potential couples.

**✗** Cons:   It can be costly and there can be quite a lot of ghosting – in other words, when you send messages and get nothing back, like the customer has vanished.

## DO WEDDING DIRECTORIES WORK?

It's the age-old debate and the answer is different for everyone. I have clients who never use directories and have successful businesses. I have others who get thousands of pounds worth of work from directories every single year. The main question you need to answer is: 'Will I get a return on my investment?'

## DO YOUR RESEARCH

There are many wedding directories across the globe and not all are created equal. Never sign up because someone contacted you out of the blue with a great offer.

Always take time to do your research. If a directory looks like a good option, then ask plenty of questions. What demographic of couples are using their site? How many website users do they have each month? Can they share some success stories with you? Ask industry peers if they have worked with a directory before to check it's legitimate. Work out how many weddings you will need to book through the site to start making that important return on investment.

## USE ALL THE TOOLS AND KEEP IT UPDATED

Once you take the plunge to invest in a site, you need to do everything you can to ensure it works. Take time putting together your listing and ask for help from your account manager to ensure you are giving it the best chance of succeeding. Ensure you have great imagery, a clear description, links to your website and social pages, and plenty of testimonials to give social proof. Ensure you are using the tools each site has on offer. Otherwise, you may be missing out on something important.

Keep an eye on your listing throughout the year, change the images and keep the text fresh if something in your business changes. If you are not getting the number of enquiries you were hoping for, get in touch with your account manager and ask what they can do to help you. It's in their best interest for the listing to work for you so that you want to become a repeat customer.

## FOLLOW UP QUICKLY AND WITH A SHORT MESSAGE

When an enquiry does come through from a listing site, it's best to reply as quickly as you can. The longer it takes you to get back to the couple, the more likely they are to have already gone with someone else. Have a template message saved to your phone and/or computer that you can reply with and just fluff up a little bit with any specific details.

Keep the first message short – don't overwhelm them with information. Give them a clear next step such as,

'Here's a link to my diary, book a call.' A short, easy-to-answer question is also a great way to end the email, to give them a reason to reply.

## WHY DO WE GET GHOSTED?

Directories are a numbers game. Imagine that your listing page is a stand at an exhibition. All the other wedding pros are in the same room with you, all at their own stands, and the couples are walking around, stopping to look at *every* stand to find out more information. It's the same online. When they are looking on a site for a photobooth, for example, they may well look through the page of suppliers that are local to them and request more information from quite a view different businesses in quick succession. After all, it only takes a couple of clicks. They finish their wedding admin and go off to get on with their day.

Now what do you think happens when they come back to their emails later that day? All of those photobooth companies have come back to them with information, pricing and photos. And guess what they feel now? Completely overwhelmed, that's what. 'How can we get back to everyone?' they think. 'This now feels like a huge task.' And it's easier to ignore most of the emails and just go with the one that makes sense (or that they opened first).

## DON'T TAKE IT PERSONALLY – AND BE THE ONE WHO FOLLOWS UP

Now you understand how the couples are feeling, it's time to realise that it's not personal when they don't get back to you. They have just drowned themselves in admin. When you are first to reply or you reply with an easy-to-read, short email, you are increasing your chances of getting a response. Once you have sent your first email, don't leave it there. Follow up two or three times over the next week with short emails, simple questions and clear next steps. If you are the only wedding pro following up, you will start to stand out in the crowded inbox.

If you get nothing back and you have followed up a number of times, just let it go. It's likely that it's not anything you did, they probably just went in a different direction, or they decided you were not a good fit for them. Don't dwell on it for too long. Just move on.

## REMEMBER THE ADDITIONAL BENEFITS

Wedding directories are used by many couples as a launch pad. The couples use the sites to narrow down their decisions but then make the enquiry via social media or your website. This can mean it is not always easy to attribute leads directly to specific platforms. Tracking your return on investment can be tricky, so it's worth also paying attention to the broader benefits that directories can bring. Many of these sites offer additional opportunities that are worth paying attention to, such as social media exposure, high-quality links back to your website, blog features and industry events such as networking and awards nights. When reviewing your presence on these websites, ask yourself whether you are making the most of these additional opportunities and whether they are positively impacting your business.

## DON'T WAIT FOR RENEWAL DAY

Whenever I speak to a client who says, 'Directories never work for me', I always ask them to explain their thought process. Quite often I hear the same story. They signed up on a deal, threw together a quick listing and after twelve months, when renewal time came up, they quit.

If you want a marketing avenue to work for you, you need to invest time and energy into it. Review your metrics quarterly and don't be afraid to ask your account manager to do more for you. Attend training or listen to podcasts on how to make the most of your listing. If you want to be good at something, you need to put the work in. Ask your account manager if they have social media campaigns or website articles that you can be part of to make the most of your investment. Renewal day is too late to make these requests. Keep on top of it all year round.

## 4. Wedding shows

✔ Pros:   In-person connection and the potential to meet lots of 'ideal couples'.

✘ Cons:   They can be costly and can involve long, tiring days.

I *love* a wedding show. When I had my videography business, it was one of the first things I invested in attending. I spent ages thinking through my stand, purchased cupcakes with my logo on to attract attention and practised what I was going to say. I loved being able to talk to numerous couples about my business and how I could help them. I collected lots of email addresses. I also discovered that quite a few people come to these events, despite not actually being engaged or planning a wedding – they are just nosey!

I realised quickly that being charismatic and engaging was a lot more enticing than the people sitting behind their stands on their phones. I also realised that not being at my stand encouraged more people to stop and look (more on that later). I booked one wedding from my first wedding show which more than paid for my stand and I was on cloud 9!

### THE MISTAKES!

Despite making a profit from the first wedding show I attended, I quickly realised I had made some mistakes.

I couldn't read the handwriting. I collected forty-eight email addresses from that first show but I quickly realised that the pad-and-pen approach was problematic as I couldn't read the handwriting! The number of emails that bounced back was disproportionate and I had to write off some of them completely. At the end of a long day, it took me far too long to type all the email addresses into my computer to follow up, and some of the follow-up didn't happen until nearly a week later. In that moment, I promised myself I would never collect email addresses on paper again! I'll tell you later in this chapter how I do this now.

I forgot to ask the wedding date. It was a rookie error but I forgot to ask anyone when they were actually getting married, so I had no way of prioritising leads or knowing when the wedding day had passed. I couldn't tell whether the leads were planning their weddings three years in advance or next summer or even if they had a date at all.

I realised that knowledge was power when it came to deciding whether or not a wedding show was worth doing again.

## CHOOSING THE RIGHT SHOW FOR YOU

Wedding shows come in many shapes and sizes, from local venue open days to huge national exhibitions. There are 'mainstream' shows and also wedding shows for a variety of different niches. There are shows at football stadiums, shopping centres, exhibition halls and even in marquees in fields. If you want to invest in a show, first up you need to do your research.

1.  Which show are your ideal couples most likely to attend?

2.  What is the average footfall for the show?

3.  How many of each supplier type will be in attendance?

4.  How big will your stand be and what is included?

5.  How much will you be charged to attend?

6.  Do you need to pay additional fees for power or wi-fi?

7.  Are there additional areas you can get involved in such as a catwalk show or a gift bag for visitors?

8.  Where will they be marketing the show to ensure they get the footfall on the day?

Wedding shows typically happen in the spring and autumn, so try to attend as many of the shows as you can before deciding which ones to invest your money in. This will give you a feel for the crowd size, the types of businesses and couples attending, and the layout.

Use them as an opportunity to network and chat with the exhibitors who are there to see how they are finding the show so far. It's great market research. Once you identify a show that's a good fit for you, do the maths and work out how many bookings you will need to take to make a healthy return on investment – this will be your target.

## IT'S HARD TO GET A SPACE

You may identify a show you want to exhibit at and then discover they don't have space. Particular supplier categories such as photography can find it harder to get a space, as the shows will often limit how many can be at any show and they will always go back to their loyal customers first.

If this is a barrier you are coming up against, see it as a goal to achieve rather than a block in your way. Whenever someone tells me 'I can't do something', it always makes me more determined to find a way to prove them wrong. If there is no space, ask to be put on a reserve list. Find out if there are other ways to get involved such as contributing to the gift bags or speaking on stage. If you have something to offer the show organiser, such as writing a review of the show, promoting it on your social media or even going to take promotional photos or videos for them, this can be a great way to start to build a business relationship.

Attend the show in question, even if you are not exhibiting, introduce yourself to the staff team (if they don't look too stressed) and share your experiences on social media. All of these ideas will make you memorable and stand out from the crowd.

Finally, be ready to stand in at short notice. If the date is free in your diary, ensure the organiser knows you are happy to be first back-up if they are let down. It's surprising how often a wedding pro doesn't show up at a wedding show, despite booking the stand. An empty space is the show organiser's worst nightmare!

Persistence without being annoying is key. One of my clients had been trying to get into a venue open day for some time, but they were always full. He always suggested they call him if they got let down because he would be happy to be the back-up. For months, nothing came of it, until one Sunday morning he got the 'back-up' call. He cancelled his plans and appeared at the venue with his set-up within an hour. The venue was so thankful and now he is asked back every time.

It's never impossible to get the space, you just have to be willing not to give up.

## PREPARING FOR THE SHOW

Once you have your space booked, it's time to start planning. Having a stand that is visually engaging and appealing is key to attracting attention. I am a big fan of avoiding the traditional stand-around-the-table set-up. It's certainly easy to plonk everything on the table provided by the venue and stick up a pop-up banner on the regulation stand – but it won't distinguish you from everyone else. Instead, bring in your own furniture to make the space look visually interesting. Ensure you have your business logo printed on a board that can be hung behind your stand – either on a standalone frame or attached to the exhibition booth space given to you. Make sure that it is high up so that it can be seen from a distance, and think about fun ways that you could attract attention.

I once spotted a stand that had a giant bath filled with white balloons. People were getting in the bath and taking selfies. It definitely caught my attention and made me go over to have a look. When I arrived at the stand, I saw that they were wedding planners. The point of the bath was to show that you could relax while they did all the hard work planning the wedding. It was a great piece of marketing and attracted a lot of attention. Nobody else had come along to the show with a full-size bathtub!!

While thinking of out-of-the-box ideas, think about how you could make your stand interactive or demonstrate what you do. When I got engaged, I couldn't wait to go to the local wedding show with my best friend. In my mind, it was going to be a really fun day out, immersing myself in wedding planning. When I walked in, I was surprised to find lots of people standing behind tables, handing out flyers and trying to convince me to stop and talk. It wasn't the fun experience I had imagined – quite the opposite.

When thinking about your offering, consider how you could get closer to that exciting experience. Could you offer hair and make-up trials to demonstrate what you do? Perhaps you could create a place for people to sit and eat cake, or attract people over with a big 'spin to win' wheel. Put yourselves in the shoes of the customers. What would make you stop or attract your attention?

You may want to consider taking an assistant or two with you on a show day. The size and scale of the show will determine how many people you will need. Show days are long and you don't want to miss leads while you take a break for lunch, or miss a lead because you are talking to another couple.

## ON THE DAY – MAKING THE MOST OF THE OPPORTUNITY

There are two main objectives when exhibiting at any wedding show:

1.  Start as many conversations as possible.

2.  Collect as many contact details as you can.

As you head into a show day, set yourself a personal target of how many new contacts you want to end the day with. Once you have your target, plan a small reward for yourself to celebrate if you hit it. Maybe ending the night with a doughnut or a takeaway? A small target will give you something to focus on and will keep you and your team motivated through the day, even when you feel exhausted.

## START CONVERSATIONS

If you have created an interactive experience, starting conversations will be easy because you have something to offer them other than a flyer and a sales pitch. Ask open, friendly questions: How are you finding your wedding planning? What are you hoping to get from the show today? Is there anything you are stuck with when it comes to your planning? Getting people relaxed and chatting will make talking about what you do a whole lot easier than jumping in with a sales pitch.

If starting a conversation feels challenging or awkward, try my 'walking away from the stand' trick. Sitting behind your table or scrolling on your phone can unintentionally act as a repellent. People often keep walking, fearing you might pounce on them if they stop. And the result is that you leave discouraged, feeling like the day was a waste of time and money.

If this is you, then try my technique that I teach the more introverted pros I work with. Wander away from your stand, go and look at something nearby, or busy yourself out of sight – but keep one eye on your area. When your stand is empty, visitors often feel safer to stop and browse. Give them a few moments to look and then wander back and ask if they need any help. This is a natural way to start a conversation without feeling like you have to attract them over.

## COLLECT THE DETAILS

'Have a think about it and get in touch if you are interested.' Finishing your conversation like this is the worst way you could end an interaction at a wedding show. You are putting all the power in the hands of the couple and letting your leads wander off, with no way of ever following up.

Wedding shows are overwhelming, couples meet multiple pros and venues in a short period of time, collect piles of business cards, and often don't remember which business was which. We need to help them through this process, which is why it's our job to follow up.

## GIVE THEM A REASON TO LEAVE THEIR DETAILS

An email address is a commodity. We are more likely to give our email address away if we get something valuable in return. If you want to collect lots of email addresses at a wedding show, you need to give them a good reason to share it. A competition prize, a special offer (added value, not discounting), a helpful guide or a video series are all good ways to encourage someone to leave their email address with you.

Ahead of the show, set up a landing page inside your email marketing system (a page that simply contains a contact form) which you can access from your tablet. You can set this up inside your email marketing software – as mentioned earlier, I recommend Mailerlite. It allows you to collect people's details securely and can also automate the responses and follow-up emails.

Your email marketing software is the easiest and most time-efficient way to collect potential leads. The tablet means you avoid the illegible handwriting. The set-up ahead of the show allows you to follow up with the couple immediately rather than typing all the emails up later that night or the following day. Ensure you include a clear statement on your sign-up form – it should make it clear that submitting the form means they agree to hear more from your business. This will ensure you are GDPR-compliant.

Now, when you are having your conversation, you can drop in that you have a prize draw, or a great resource, and would they like to leave their details? Now just hand them the iPad and let them do the rest.

Once they submit the form, it will pop up with a thank-you page. You can set this to let them know they will already have an email from you in their inbox and to check their spam folder if they can't see it. The chances are that you will be the first person they hear from, while everyone else waits until later that evening, or later in the week, to send their follow-ups.

## WRITING THE FIRST FOLLOW-UP EMAIL

The initial email, which you set to send as soon as they submit the form, should include the following:

1.  A photo of you – because, by the end of the day, they won't remember who they spoke to or which business it was. A photo of you will jog their memory and remind them of the conversation.

2.  A short message about how it was great to chat with them and a link or reminder of whatever you promised them in return for their email address.

3.  A clear call to action about what you want them to do next. For example, check my prices here and then book a call here. Or reply to this email if you want to find out more about working together.

4.  A mention that you will be in touch with some helpful tips and follow up over the next couple of days.

## EMAIL SEQUENCE

Your email marketing system will allow you to plan all your follow-up emails ahead of the show, so that they go out without you having to do a thing. Whenever I build email sequences for my clients, I tend to follow this pattern:

1.  Email 1: Instantly (details as above).

2.  Email 2: The day after the show: 'It was great to meet you yesterday.' Add some value and a clear call to action.

3.  Email 3: Two to three days later: 'Hopefully by now you have had time to look over everything.' Add some value and a clear call to action.

4.  Email 4: One week after the show: 'It's been a week since we met. Let me know if you are interested or if you have decided to go in a different direction.'

Once they have worked their way through the system, they can land in your overall email marketing group. Then you can contact them regularly with a newsletter or monthly updates.

An effective follow-up campaign is more likely to lead to conversions. As I once heard someone say, 'Even when someone deletes your email, they remember your name as they press delete.'

## THE HOT/COLD METHOD

For a more advanced approach at a show, I recommend the hot/cold method. This is where you have two ends to your conversation, depending on how it's going. As you are talking, you need to decide whether to send them down a 'hot path' or a 'cold path'.

The 'cold path' is for people who are vaguely interested, but not asking many in-depth questions or talking in detail about their wedding day. Perhaps they are just browsing or not yet committed on a wedding date. If that's the case, then you will send them down the cold route, exactly as detailed above with an automated follow-up sequence and some kind of value to get them to fill in their email address.

The 'hot path' is for people who are asking more in-depth questions, sounding genuinely interested in working with you for their day and asking about pricing or your availability. These are hot leads, and we want to give them a more personalised follow-up experience. Instead of sending them down the cold route, collect their details in a different way: take some notes about what they have told you, such as their wedding date or venue and something memorable they have mentioned. You can do this on a notepad or pre-prepared postcard – or ask them to fill out the contact form on your website with their details and the information that you will need which you can refer to later.

Instead of sending them a standard follow-up, you are going to send a warmer, personalised email, mentioning some of the details you have noted down and encouraging them to jump on a call. This still needs to happen quickly, so send these emails during a lull in the show, or as soon as you get home that evening.

**SUPER-HOT LEADS**

Occasionally, a couple want to book you there and then, so it's important you have a process to do this. You don't want to send them away because you are not prepared. Although it's often the exception rather than the rule, these opportunities do happen and we want to leap at them.

Always have your availability calendar with you at the show and a method of taking payment (either by bank transfer or a card reader). If they are keen and showing strong buying signals, don't send them away and follow up with an email, instead ask if they would like to reserve the date and pay a deposit to secure it. You could even book in a phone appointment or follow-up call while they are with you. Don't be afraid to sell. If someone wants to buy, let them.

Wedding shows should be fun and result in lots of new leads into your business. If you are at the right show, you should also see a healthy return on investment. If shows haven't worked for you up to this point, review how much of what I have mentioned above you have implemented – or if there are changes you could make to find more success.

I once spoke at the National Wedding Show and got chatting to a photographer who was exhibiting close to the stage. They were not having a successful show and said they were wondering why they had invested so much to be there. I had a fifteen-minute break, so I did a quick review of their stand and what they were offering. I gently shared my advice – they had no strategy, no targets and no way of collecting details.

That evening, the photographer went home and created an email sequence and new ideas for their stand. The next day at the show, they turned up with new energy and a new plan. And guess what? They started collecting leads. People now had a reason to stop and the photographer started to have more sales conversations.

They even took two on-the-day bookings. When a show doesn't work for you, it may not be the show that is the problem. It may just be that you need a fresh approach.

## 5. PR and media

✔ Pros:  It gives you a competitive edge and gives you authority.

✘ Cons:  It can be time-consuming to chase down leads and compile pitches.

The final strategy I want to share with you in this chapter is PR and media. When I mention PR and media, I am referring to magazines, television and radio appearances, and industry blogs.

If you want to stand out from the crowd, a strong PR presence can set you apart and give you authority in your field. So how can you achieve it?

Last week, I got an Instagram message asking if I wanted to pay $500 to appear in the *Chicago Times* list of 'Entrepreneurs who are redefining success'. My response? I don't pay for PR opportunities. Having spent six years working in the television and radio industry, I know that there are ways you can appear in the media without having to pay a penny.

## YOU NEED A STORY

Journalists in a multimedia world are on the look-out for content 24/7. News channels and online magazines are frequently updated and they all need fresh ideas and perspectives.

If you want to appear in publications, you need to find an angle – and owning a business doesn't constitute a story. Find the publications you want to appear in and start researching the kind of articles they publish and the stories they like to write. Every publication will have a different tone of voice and different type of article, so really understanding how they put their articles together will help you construct a story to pitch.

## PITCHING

When you come up with a concept, the next thing you need to do is find the journalist and send an email to pitch. Your easiest routes to press are via local newspapers or radio stations, so these are a good place to practise and to get your first media exposure.

I have appeared in my local paper numerous times because they love anything with a local angle that celebrates good things happening in an area. Your pitch email needs to be short and to the point, so it's easy for the journalist to read. They have busy inboxes.

Here's an example of a pitch I sent to my local paper and radio station which resulted in press coverage:

Subject line: Story idea: 'Local businesswoman wins international wedding award'

Email:

Hi X

I would love to pitch a story idea to you for X publication:

Local businesswoman wins international wedding award. Becca Pountney from X has just been awarded with X prize. The local mum of two has been running her wedding business for the last five years and was thrilled to receive the accolade.

I'm happy to provide more information and comments if you are interested in featuring the story.

I look forward to hearing from you.

Becca Pountney

You may get ignored. You may need to send a follow-up. But, as they say, if you don't ask, you don't get, so it's worth giving it a try.

## PROVIDING COMMENT FOR STORIES

Journalists are always looking for comments on stories they are working on. Looking online at the #journorequest or being in Facebook groups where journalists are looking for comments can be a good place to start. You can also sign up to an email called HARO (Help A Reporter Out) where they send you requests daily. There's often a lot of irrelevant items to sift through, but you do occasionally find wedding-related stories or items around being an entrepreneur.

## WEDDING BLOGS

There are multiple publications online that specialise in wedding content and will be looking for new angles, styled photoshoots and interesting stories. Follow the guidelines above and do your research, but there are plenty of ways to be featured without paying for an advert or a listing. If you are a paying client, you are more likely to get featured. However, don't let that hold you back, as it's not always the case.

## WHAT ARE THE BENEFITS OF BEING FEATURED?

Being featured in the press may lead to enquiries, but the bigger benefit is the authority it brings. Talking about being featured in Forbes, Vogue or on the BBC shows your future couples that you are an expert in your field and that they can trust you. Media features can set you apart from the competition and give you the edge in a crowded market.

## Let's get practical

*Narrow it down and start to improve one area.*

As I bring this chapter to a close, I want to remind you that you can't do it all right away. Now you have read about all of the different forms of marketing, it's time to narrow it down and start to improve one area.

1.  Complete some market research to work out where your ideal clients are spending their time and planning their wedding.

2.  Highlight two or three of the marketing ideas I have shared above that you feel comfortable with and that you think could work for you. Work out the investment and what you would need to gain to see a return on investment.

3.  Get to work, don't let perfectionism hold you back, remember that 'done is better than perfect' and marketing is about being visible. So, start getting visible and improve it over time.

# SIMPLIFY
Untangle your processes

When I was younger, I used to love the computer game Lemmings. It was a simple concept – crowds of lemmings would be dropped at the start of the game and they would all follow each other along. As the player, you had to help the lemmings navigate the course from start to finish, without ending in peril. But make the wrong decision and all of your lemmings would walk themselves off the edge of the cliff and it was game over. Each step of their journey was down to me as the player and I had to lead them step-by-step to safety.

When we are trying to guide our potential customers through a buying process, they are like those little lemmings. They don't know where to go. They don't know how it works, and it's our job to gently lead them through the buying and planning process. We live inside our business day in, day out, so everything seems obvious to us, but to our potential clients it's not. When they work with multiple wedding pros who all have different processes, it doesn't take long for them to get confused.

## Simplicity is key

Could a seven-year-old understand your booking process? If I asked you to explain to a group of seven-year-old children how to work with you, would they be able to understand or would they be left totally confused? This little test is a good way to see how complex your systems have become.

When my children were seven, they could understand how to purchase something from Amazon or order a pizza from Dominos, because the processes are so simple. In just a couple of clicks the item is yours. Online retailers are updating their stores to include one-click buying to make purchasing simpler for the customer. Why are they doing this? They know the simpler the buying process, the more purchases a customer will make.

*Could a seven-year-old understand your booking process?*

I have lost count of the number of conversations with wedding venues and wedding pros who have explained their over-complicated booking processes to me – they made even my experienced head spin. Why do I have to fill out three separate forms just to come and tour the venue? Why do I fill out a form on your website and then immediately get sent another form asking for similar information? Each step in the journey is a place where those lemmings may fall off a cliff, so we need to make that journey easier for them.

## Reviewing your processes

In order to simplify your customers journey, you first need to identify what your processes look like right now. Grab a pen and paper and write out everything a customer has to take between discovering you exist and booking you for their wedding day. Here's an example of how your written list could look.

1. Customer discovers the business on Google, social media or via a recommendation.

2. Customer looks at my website and researches my offerings and prices.

3. Customer clicks on a button to contact the business.

4. Customer fills out enquiry form.

5. I receive form and now send them an email back asking for more information.

6. Customer sends more information.

7. I ask customer if they would like to have a chat and ask when they are free.

8. Customer emails to say they are free Saturday morning this week.

9. I reply to customer explaining I have a wedding Saturday but could do Sunday.

10. Customer replies to say they can make Sunday.

11. I reply with a Zoom link.

12. I talk to customer for thirty minutes and say I will send over a proposal next week.

13. I write proposal and send it to customer.

14. I chase customer as haven't heard anything.

15. Customer replies with more queries.

16. I reply with answers to queries and ask if customer would like to book.

17. Customer replies to say that they would like to book.

18. I send an email with a contract to be printed and signed and an invoice to be paid.

19. Customer prints and signs contract, returns signed contract and makes payment.

20. I send a booking confirmation and the process can begin.

Now you have your process written out, it's time to review it with a fresh perspective. How many opportunities are there for your lemmings to walk off the cliff and never speak to you again? How drawn out is your process? How could it be made easier?

## Time to simplify!

Now you have your list, it's time for us to start stripping it down and simplifying it. There are a few ways of doing this. First, we need to look for unnecessary steps and see if they can be removed. Are there forms that could be combined? Could you have more information available on your site so that you don't have to send it afterwards? Are there areas where you could combine the steps to make the journey shorter?

Once you have identified unnecessary steps, we now need to look at simplifying or automating the steps you still require. Could an automated reply go straight to the customer as soon as they fill out your contact form? Could you set up an online appointment calendar so that they can book a time to talk so that you don't have to go back and forth about dates? Could you use a system so that your contracts can be signed digitally or payments made online? Every step you can remove or simplify allows for a smoother experience for your customers.

## Share the steps with your couples

As humans, we don't like to do things we don't under-stand. New experiences can be nerve-wracking, and if we don't understand a process we often avoid it. I have never been in a betting shop. The thought of it terrifies me. If I were to walk into one tomorrow, I would feel like a fish out of water. I have no idea what happens inside those four walls, what the process is in order to make a bet or what the correct etiquette is. If someone were to walk me through it or explain it to me once, the visit would feel a whole lot easier.

When couples get engaged, the process is confusing and often alien to them. A simple guide on your website of how to work with you can go a long way. It takes the mystery and the worry away and ensures they know what happens next. I always advise my clients to add a simple three- or four-step process to their website where it is visible and clearly described with icons or graphics.

I had a wedding stationery client a couple of years ago who added the following guide to her website:

Step one: Fill out my enquiry form below.

Step two: We'll get on a call and plan your stationery.

Step three: I will make your designs and deliver them twelve weeks before the wedding date.

It was a very simple change and the steps seemed obvious to her, but it made a big difference to the couples looking at her website. As a direct result, she saw an increase in enquiries and more of the enquiries turned into sales – all because she mapped out the process and made it clear from the start. Could you simplify your

*Add a simple three- or four-step process to your website.*

process into three or four clear steps and put them on your website?

Now you have your process mapped out and clear, it's time to do a deep-dive analysis on your current situation, to identify how you can simplify things for your potential clients.

## Where are the leaks?

Another way to describe your customers' journey is a 'sales funnel'. The funnel describes the shape of the pathway that customers journey with you. You will inevitably lose some leads along the way. As some potential customers drop off, the size of the funnel narrows. You may have ten prospects at the start of the sales funnel but perhaps only three or four will actually end up working with you. If you want more sales, it usually means you need more people entering the top of your sales funnel.

Whenever I review a business, I usually start by analysing the state of the sales funnel. If we can find the leak, it's easier to find the fix. You may think your biggest problem is sales, but it may actually be that your initial enquiries are low because you are marketing to the wrong people. If that's the case, a full day of sales training, as great as it may be, won't fix the issue.

To diagnose the leak in your funnel, you first need to draw it out, using your simplified customer journey that you created earlier. It should look something like the below example.

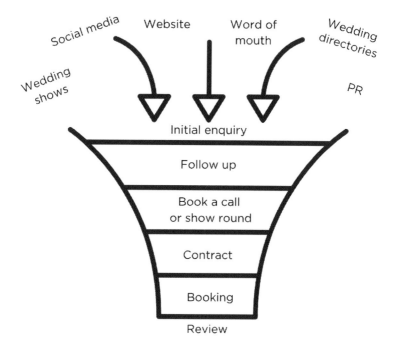

Social media  Website  Word of mouth  Wedding directories

Wedding shows  PR

Initial enquiry

Follow up

Book a call or show round

Contract

Booking

Review

Now you have the funnel, you need to work out where the leaks are by looking at your recent numbers. There are five stages where your funnel might spring a leak.

## STAGE 1

Over the last three months, how visible have you been? Are you gaining new social followers or meeting new people at wedding shows? Are you being found on Google and bringing new visitors to your website? This is often one of the biggest problem areas. If people don't know you exist, then you are never going to move them further down the sales funnel.

*Action:* If Stage 1 is your leak, go back and look over the previous two chapters. Plan to up your visibility and let more of the right people know about your business. The more people that know you exist, the more enquiries you should receive.

## STAGE 2

How many enquiries have you had into your business over the last three months? Do you have a steady stream of new leads filling out your enquiry form or dropping into your DMs? If you have lots of people visiting your site, showing an interest in your business or engaging on social media but a very low level of enquiries, then this could be your problem area.

*Action:* If Stage 2 is your leak, it's time to review the information on your site and see if you are putting people off. Do you have clear, available pricing on your website? Do you have examples of your previous work and testimonials? Is it clear what your customers need to do next in order to make an enquiry – or is it too complicated? We know that the internet-savvy generation of engaged couples are good at doing their research. That means they are looking at your website and social media presence to weigh up whether to get in touch or not. If they are looking, but not enquiring, then something is putting them off. It's up to you to identify what that is.

**STAGE 3**

How many of the enquiries that came into your business over the last three months resulted in a call or show round? Write down a percentage so that you know what proportion converted into that next stage. For example, if you had ten enquiries and two of them resulted in a call, it would be a 20% conversion rate at Stage 3.

*Action:* If Stage 3 is your leak, then it's likely that you are experiencing ghosting, which feels very frustrating. If this is where your leaks are happening, then there are a number of things to review in your process.

- Where are the enquiries coming from and are they quality enquiries?

- How quickly are you responding to the initial enquiry? The faster you respond, the more likely you are to start a conversation.

- Are your replies too long and overwhelming? When a couple sends an enquiry, they want a simple, clear response back, not a 1,000-word essay that they probably will just delete.

- Are you giving them a simple next step or an easy question to answer? If they don't know what to do next, they will likely do nothing.

- Is this the first time they are seeing your prices? If they couldn't find your prices online and then see them in this first response, it may be that they realised you are out of budget, so they have now counted you out.

- Is your next step simple to complete? Stating 'If you are interested in going ahead, then please book a time for us to talk in more detail' or 'Come and visit our venue – here is a link to our diary' are both clear and easy ways to encourage them onto the next step.

- Are you giving too many options? Customers are often paralysed by choice, so give them one simple call to action in your email. Choices can lead to indecision.

**STAGE 4**

How many of your calls or show rounds converted into closing the sale? Once again, write down a percentage so you can see the conversion rate from calls and show rounds into sales.

*Action:* If Stage 4 is your leak, then this sounds like a sales problem. By the time someone gives up their day to speak or meet with you, they are a very warm lead and it's down to you to close the sale with them. If this is your leaky area, then pay careful attention to the next chapter, where I am going to talk more in depth about how to confidently close the sale.

## STAGE 5

The final stage that may be causing you a problem is right at the end. Perhaps you rarely get reviews or your couples rarely recommend you to their friends. If this is true for you, then I want you to reflect on your customer service and relationship building with the couple.

*Action:* Set the couple up for the fact you are going to ask for a review before you ask for it. Explain to them how reviews make a big difference to you in your business, so that when you get in touch following the wedding, they are primed and ready to go.

Ensure you make it easy for a review to be left. Send them one simple link. Don't ask for a review to be left in five different places. Decide on your focus and direct them there. You may also need to remind a couple a few times about the review as they will be back from their honeymoon and back to the busyness of life. How many times have you gone to reply to a message or email only to be distracted by a knock at the door or a phone call and then it completely slips your mind? You may need to send a gentle reminder if they have said they will be willing to leave you one.

Reviews can take many forms. A handwritten card or a text to say thank you can also be used as a testimonial in the future. Take a photo or a screenshot and start a folder on your phone called 'Kind words or testimonials'. These can be uploaded to your social media, inserted into emails or added to your website. They all help showcase why you are worth booking.

Now you have your customer journey mapped out and you have identified the gaps, it's time to put the work in to fix them. Keep an eye on your numbers from month to month and start to track enquiries, calls and conversions on a monthly basis. Review them each quarter. If you can increase conversion at each stage by just 1% by making small changes, it will positively impact your revenue and keep driving your business forward. Your plans don't have to be perfect. Just get started on one thing.

## Let's get practical

There are a lot of action steps in this chapter, so let's break them down:

1. Write out your customer journey and simplify it by removing steps or adding automation.

2. Add a three- or four-step booking process to your website.

3. Map out your funnel and uncover the leaks.

4.  Work out how to fix the leaks.

5.  Monitor your conversion numbers to see how the small changes have an impact over time.

# SALES

Close the deal

I hate selling. It feels sleazy and I like to give people time to think about what they are buying. I don't want them to feel any pressure, so I will wait until they are ready.

Raise your hand if these words have ever come out of your mouth. We have all experienced poor sales practices and it often leads to a huge fear of selling. As a business owner, it's inevitable that you will have to make sales, otherwise you will not survive very long. Even the most creative entrepreneur who decorates cakes or designs bouquets for a living has to learn to make sales, otherwise they are going to go out of business very fast.

## What does sales mean to you?

Before I talk about how to close the sale, I first need you to shift your perspective on what selling is. If you are picturing the estate agent trying to sell you a property that is clearly no good, or the furniture salesman pushing you to buy a sofa *today* before their amazing sale ends, then you are not going to feel keen to discuss the subject. Instead, we need to reframe our mindsets when it comes to selling. The reason those examples feel so uncomfortable to us is usually because they are trying to sell us something that we don't want or need in that moment.

Let's look at an alternative example. I am at home working and it's lunch time. I go to my bread bin and realise the last of the bread was used for the children's packed lunch that morning. I really want a sandwich and I'm hungry, so I nip over to the shop to buy a loaf of bread. If I take the bread to the counter and the shop worker says, 'Do you need some time to consider this purchase? Please don't feel any pressure to buy. Go away and think about it and come back later', I would find that incredibly frustrating. I am hungry. I know I want the bread, now please just sell me the bread! When I go to buy bread, there is never an instance where I am going to feel like the shop worker is trying to pressure me to buy. They are selling me something I want and need.

So often I hear wedding pros and wedding venues falling into that trap. They are so worried about being too pushy that they swing to the opposite extreme. In trying to avoid putting pressure on people, they fail to close the transaction confidently. And by leaving potential customers too much room to go away and think about it, they miss the opportunity.

## What is sales?

In its purest form, sales is just selling someone a solution to a problem that they have.

I'm tired and on my way to work. I want to buy a coffee.

I have accidentally locked myself out. I want to pay a locksmith to let me in.

Whenever I paint my nails, they smudge and look awful. I want to pay a professional so my nails look great at my next event.

I want to invite 100 friends to celebrate our wedding but our house is way too small, so I need to hire a venue instead.

I want a beautiful cake that will serve 100 guests but I don't have the skill or time to make it myself, so I will pay someone who can.

*Sales is selling someone a solution to a problem that they have.*

When we realise we are solving a problem for our customers, we realise that selling is actually just giving them a helping hand. In fact, we are doing them a disservice by *not* selling to them as they need our help.

## Why people don't buy

It's Saturday morning and I'm heading out to the shops. I don't have a particular item that I am shopping for – I'm just browsing today and hoping to find something I like.

I start at my favourite store, but as I get closer I can see that it is closed today due to staff illness. *Frustrating*, I think, *I always find something I like in there*. I move onto the next store, but the clothes just don't look very 'me'. I'm not a fan of this season's styles and so I swiftly exit. I pop briefly into a store that I love but definitely cannot afford. I find lots of lovely items, but a few glances at the price tags and I remember why this store is usually one I avoid. I smile at the shop assistant and glide right on out of there. I stop for a coffee at my favourite coffee shop. I always need coffee and I know I can rely on them to always make a lovely drink, plus they scan my rewards card which means I am one step closer to a free drink – yay!

I decide to stop in one final store before going home. It's a big one and I find quite a few items that I like. I gather them up and take them to the changing room. The queue is huge, but I decide this time it's worth the wait. I finally get into my tiny cubicle with the terrible lighting and try on a few of the outfits. One is too tight, one is too large and one looks great, but the size isn't quite right. I call the shop assistant over and ask if they could get it for me in an alternative size. 'Sorry,' she says, 'that's the only size we have left.' Disgruntled, I bundle all the clothes back up and hand them over, and off I go home. The only thing I bought all day was that coffee!

Have you ever had a day like this? Look back over the story and work out all of the things that stopped me from making a purchase. I had money to spend, but there were multiple barriers to the sale – did you spot them?

According to American author Zig Ziglar, every sale has five basic obstacles:

1.   No need

2.   No money

3.   No hurry

4.   No desire

5.   No trust

If our customers encounter one of these obstacles, then the chances are that we won't make the sale, so let's look at how we can work to ensure we have the best chance of closing the deal.

## 1. NO NEED

In your marketing, you need to ensure you are explaining all the benefits of your product and why you are not a 'nice to have' but a 'need to have'. I often hear wedding pros describing themselves as an 'extra' if people have the budget, but you are going to lose out on the sale if the couple don't see you as essential.

In reality, none of our services are essential to a wedding couple. It's not like food, which they need to survive – they will all get through life without wedding photos or a bouquet. Yet some parts of the market have done a great job at becoming an 'essential piece' of the wedding in the minds of the customers. It's why photographers and the wedding dress retailers are often the first businesses to be booked after the venue.

Over the last decade, I have watched certain sectors of the wedding market shift themselves from 'nice to have' to 'need to have' very effectively. When I got married in 2010, there were no photobooths, crazy golf courses or garden games. The gap between the ceremony and the meal involved my guests sitting in the sun and having a chat, and that was the case at every wedding I went to. Yet all these years later, every wedding I go to has some form of entertainment for the guests, and these businesses are popping up and evolving all over the country.

So, what has changed? Over the last decade, entertainment businesses have done an amazing job at marketing themselves as essential. They have pointed out the long gaps at weddings and how bored the guests get, and they have created solutions to overcome that. New ideas have entered the market, and the couples are worried about their wedding being less fun than everyone else's, so entertaining the guests has become an essential rather than a nice-to-have.

How can you position your business as essential rather than nice-to-have? What problems or challenges are you helping the couple to solve and how can you show them that clearly in your marketing?

## 2. NO MONEY

You may have the best marketing in the world, but if a couple don't have any money to pay you, the sale will never happen. I have all the desire in the world to fly my family first-class, but I definitely don't have the money available to make that happen. Does that mean that first class flights should be cheaper? Not at all! There are plenty of people who will pay that money. I am just not the right customer.

Ensuring you have a pricing guide on your website is the quickest way to ensure the couples who enquire have the money to pay you. When a customer sees your prices, they can filter themselves out when they realise they don't have the budget to pay you. Remember when I looked at the clothing tags and walked right out of the store. This is what couples will do when they see pricing on your website that they can't afford. This is a positive. You will save yourself time trying to sell to people who don't have the money. When you do have a call or a show round, you will already know that it isn't money that's the sales sticking point, even if that's what they say. We will talk more on pricing in chapter 8.

## 3. NO HURRY

Why is it that, when a popular band announces a concert and the ticket sales go live, thousands of people sit in a virtual queue to grab them? It's because they know that, if they wait, they will sell out and therefore they have to hurry to grab them. It's the same reason that I ordered tickets to see Santa at Lapland UK in March. The demand is such that you have to hurry to get the space or you will miss out. On the other hand, if we know there is always availability, we wait until the last moment to make the purchase. If we don't have to commit, we won't.

Although we don't want to pretend we are busier than we are, we also don't want to give the impression that we are always available, otherwise it's harder to close the sale. I once went to train the owners of a venue who said they held dates indefinitely for couples with no financial commitment – and they wondered why they never got back to them. Instead, give people a time frame: 'We will hold the date for three days, after which it will be released to other couples who may be interested in the same date.'

A few weeks ago, my daughter spotted a toy in Aldi that she wanted, and pleaded with me to buy it for her. I said no. This went on for several weeks. Each time she saw it, she begged. Each time, I said no. This weekend, we took our usual trip to Aldi and the toy was still there. But this time was different. Only one of the toys was left. All the others had been sold. She looked at me and said, 'It's the last chance. If we don't get it today, it will be gone forever. Can you at least buy it and save it until my birthday so I don't miss out?' Suddenly my weekly no became a yes, because the urgency level had shifted. I have no idea if they had all sold, or if they had five hundred more hidden round the back – but I didn't take the risk and I made the purchase (and have hidden it until her birthday).

If you only have one peak date left this summer, tell people. If you are already having enquiries for two years' time, tell people. When something is too readily available, we have no reason to book it early, so let's give your couples a reason to close the sale.

## 4. NO DESIRE

When a sales call doesn't end up in a booking, it can feel personal. We may reflect and assume it must be about price, or something we did. However, it could just be personal choice – the desire to purchase wasn't great enough. Desire is subjective and therefore it is one of the more difficult sales obstacles to overcome.

Imagine a couple have spoken with two wedding photographers. They have almost identical pricing and the couple get on with both of them. The couple go away and look at the portfolios of both and decide that they prefer the work of photographer A and book her. What could photographer B have done to change their mind? Not a lot. Sometimes they just prefer the other person's work and it's not personal.

So how can we influence desire? Although taste is subjective, there are some things we can do to try and make an impression. Ensure your work is photographed professionally so that it is visually appealing. Whenever I go to an amazing hotel, I take a photo of the room I'm staying in, yet it never looks anywhere near as good as the marketing images of the room that they use online. If the hotel used my phone images to advertise online, I'm fairly sure they would see a decline in bookings. If you want to give yourself the best chance of being chosen, every photo of your work needs to wow your clients. Take some time to look over your images on your website and social media – is it time to refresh them to give you the wow factor?

If you are welcoming people to your venue or an in-person meeting, you need to give them a great first impression. A couple will know almost instantly when they walk into your venue whether they fall in love with it or not. There are ways you can increase the desire by giving them an amazing customer experience, greeting them personally on arrival and having the venue set up in a way that shows it off and allows them to imagine how it could look on their day.

Desire can overpower logic. When a couple fall in love with our venue or service, they will move mountains to make it work. When I got married, I knew exactly who I wanted to photograph my wedding. I had seen his work before I got engaged and immediately fell in love with his style. There were two problems: he was way out of my budget and he was very booked up. Yet I knew I *had* to have this photographer. Despite there being plenty of other choices, my desire was strong. I contacted him to find out which dates he had left and I booked my wedding date around his availability. I also explained to him that I couldn't afford his full package, so we agreed a shorter day. He would photograph the getting ready through to us sitting down for dinner, and that would only be a few hundred pounds over budget. I knew I had to make it work, so I cut back in other areas and ensured I could have him as my photographer. It was worth every penny and I still love my wedding photographs. If you can get the desire piece right, the sale will be simple.

## 5. NO TRUST

You will probably have heard the saying that for a customer to buy they first need to 'know, like and trust you'. If we don't trust the business, we are not likely to part with our money. Have you ever been looking for a service online and come across a website that looks anything but legitimate? You take one look at it, and instantly decide that's probably one to avoid. The images look poor quality, it says 'Not Secure' in the address bar and it just doesn't look very professional. How about when you find a business you like on social media and then realise they don't have a website or the links are broken?

How can you build trust with customers when they come across you online? Testimonials and reviews are essential, and the more you can collect, the better. Don't hide them away. Have them scattered across your website, ideally with an image of the couple with them. Sites which allow reviews to be left by couples, such as Google, Facebook and the directories, are a great way of gaining trust, so ensure you are gathering reviews in all of these places. Showing up with a portfolio or gallery of past work is also a great way to showcase your ability while gaining the all-important trust and showing your face online rather than hiding behind a brand.

We will always trust recommendations from our friends and family over a business we find online which is why a sale is more likely to convert when it comes via a recommendation. In the next chapter, we will be looking more deeply at how you can build these relationships to increase enquiries.

Next time you have a customer that doesn't convert, revisit your conversation in light of these five sales objections. Try and identify which of them caused the sale to cease. What can you change or learn for next time to improve your chances of conversion?

In the next section of this chapter, you will have the opportunity to choose your own adventure. OK, it's not really an adventure, but I used to really enjoy those books where you got to the bottom of the page and could make a choice about which page you went to next, depending on how you wanted the story to go.

It's time to make your choice. The next two sections are optional, and you can decide which to read based on your business. If you are a wedding business, head to Section A: The art of the sales call. If you work for or own a wedding venue, head to Section B: The art of the show round.

## Section A: The art of the sales call

Once you have a couple on a call, this is your chance to show them exactly what you do and to get that final buy in from them. Whether you meet them in person or online, the process will be similar. Each of us will have a different business to sell, but I am going to walk you through a framework which will give you the best chance to succeed in these meetings.

If you have followed the advice earlier in this book, your couple will have already got a good idea on your brand, your work, your past reviews and your pricing. If they have reviewed all of that information and made the decision to speak with you, then they have already qualified themselves. This is just the final piece of the puzzle.

## 1. GET CHATTY

Open the conversation by asking the couple some questions about themselves. It's vital that the couple feel at ease, so the sooner you can get them to relax, the better. The quickest way to help someone feel at ease is by getting them talking about something they enjoy. You don't want this to feel like a job interview, so this isn't the time to ask them specific details of their wedding planning, but instead get them talking about how they met, how they got engaged and what they imagine their day to be like.

## 2. LISTEN MORE THAN YOU SPEAK

As you speak to your couple, it will be tempting to interject and start sharing your own experience and how you can help them. But hold back. The more you listen, the more relaxed they will become and the more information you will be able to glean about what they do and don't want from their wedding day. Ask them about their concerns about the day, what they really hope for from their *florist* [insert your service in here] and what they really don't want. Listen out for any concerns they have and save them in your mind for later.

## 3. SHARE HOW YOU CAN HELP THEM

Now you have listened to what they want, you can now ask if they would like to hear how you can assist them. This is when you will share your services and how they will fit in with what they do and don't want from their wedding day. You need to weave in as much of the information as you can from what they have just shared to ensure your pitch sounds very personalised. In fact, you are assuring them that you are the right choice for them.

Let me share some examples of how this could work:

a) The couple want to book you as the florist, but they have explained they are very concerned about the flowers wilting on the day and are conscious about sustainability. When you explain your services, you could say, 'We would love to create your wedding flowers for you. We are foam free and try to source as many flowers locally as possible to keep our carbon footprint lower. We have supplied wedding flowers for hundreds of couples and know how to keep your flowers fresh so that they look great on your wedding day.'

b) The couple want you as their DJ, but they hate cheesy music and want a more relaxed vibe. You could say, 'Let me show you my packages and walk you through how I personalise the day for you so that I ensure the vibe is how you want it. Ahead of the evening, there will be an opportunity for you to submit songs you would love to hear, and those you definitely don't, so you can relax and know that song you hate isn't going to appear.'

Hopefully, you get the idea and can create a similar example for your business. You must always be truthful, but you want to ensure when you talk about your services that you include the things they want and overcome the worries they expressed in your conversation with them.

## 4. DO NOT ASK FOR THE BUDGET

On the whole, the quickest way to kill a conversation is to ask for the budget. Not only do couples often close down when asked about money, they don't always want to share. It may also be the case that they haven't worked out the budget for each supplier yet, or that budget isn't an issue. Although you don't want to ask the budget question outright, it is helpful to get an idea of how much they want to spend. This is where having packages or example pricing on your website is very helpful. You can pull the examples up and ask them which they think looks most in line with what they are looking for. Without asking for a figure, they will point at an option that fits their budget, so this gives you a great jumping off point to start talking about money in a more relaxed way.

In some circumstances, such as for a wedding planner, the conversation about money may be unavoidable. Try using different phrasing such as 'Have you considered your overall spend?' rather than asking outright about budget.

During the conversation, you do want to give some idea about the cost of working with you based on the services they are interested in. If you know an exact price, then great. But even if you don't, you will need to go away and finalise figures. Giving them a ballpark amount on the call will help you move the sale to the next phase. You will also be able to gauge from their reaction whether they are comfortable with the figures being discussed or whether they need alternative options to bring the price up or down. Here are some examples of how you can talk about pricing:

*The quickest way to kill a conversation is to ask for the budget.*

Have a look at my most popular three packages. Which one looks like it fits you the best?

I have created a cake similar to that before and it cost approximately £950, although it may be slightly under or over that depending on the details we decide on.

I will draw up two different options for you based on what we have discussed – one for £1,500 and one for £2,500 and you can see which one you prefer.

## 5. GET A 'YES', A 'NO' OR A NEXT STEP

This is the point of a call where you might panic and use the phrase, 'Go away and think about it and get back to me.' Although this feels like a comfortable solution, it is also instantly lowering your chance of making a sale by giving them no clear next step or sense of urgency. Instead, we want to ask a clear question to get a 'yes', a 'no' or a 'what next?' answer.

> Now you have seen everything and are happy with the pricing, would you like to go ahead and reserve your date?

Then pause, don't speak anymore. Wait, even if it feels uncomfortable, until they give you an answer.

If they say yes, this is great news! Now you can move straight onto finalising the sale. Explain to them exactly what will happen next and the time frame. For example:

> Great, I can't wait to work with you. I will finalise your proposal this evening and send it over in the morning along with a contract and an invoice for the first payment. I will reserve the date for you for three days to give you time to complete the paperwork. If you have any queries or changes, reply to the email and let me know.

If they say no, it's time to ask a follow-up question. What needs to happen to move that no to a yes? Finding out the objections now gives you the chance to overcome them and move forward with the sale. It may be that they say they need time to think about it or to speak with a family member. Perhaps they have another call with an alternative wedding pro that they want to do first.

If that's the case, we are not going to push them into deciding right now. Instead, you are going to agree some clear next steps with them that they are happy with. Always agree the time frame and the next method of communication. For example:

> I will send you an email now with everything we have discussed and will then follow up on Monday after you have spoken with your mum about the budget, and we can go from there.

## 6. FOLLOW UP IMMEDIATELY

As soon as the call is over, follow up immediately with an email recapping what you discussed on the call and the agreed next steps. When there is a lot of information in a conversation, we don't always remember it clearly. Having it succinctly written down, with a clear next step pathway, makes it crystal clear to everyone.

The more calls you do and the more conversions you see, the more confident you will become. These sales calls should feel like natural conversations. Think less about what you are trying to sell and more about how you can help solve their problem and be of service to them.

## Section B: The art of the show round

If you work in or own a venue, the show round or venue tour is a key part of your success rate. When a couple take the time to come and look at your space, they are ready to buy. It's your job to wow them and help them fall in love with your space.

### 1. PLAN FOR A SMOOTH ARRIVAL

Have you ever made an appointment to be somewhere that you have never been before and ended up in a complete meltdown? Perhaps the traffic was heavy or you got lost. It may be that you find the location but can't work out where to park or where the entrance to the building actually is. When this happens, you start your appointment in a stressed-out mood, and it's likely going to impact your outlook on what happens next. You don't want couples to go through this experience on their way to your venue show round, otherwise you will be on the back foot before you even get started.

A 'How to find us' guide is a great way to set your couple up for success before the show round. Brief instructions for how to find your venue, where to park and where to meet you can make all the difference. I have seen venues create short videos which walk couples through the arrival route and parking so that they can be prepared ahead of time. Perhaps you could reserve a parking space for them right outside the entrance to lower their stress levels and help them start the tour already feeling like VIPs. We want to give ourselves and our couples the most relaxed experience possible.

## 2. GIVE THEM A PERSONALISED WELCOME

When a couple book an appointment ahead of time, you don't need them to interact with the front desk on arrival. Instead, just like you would on their wedding day, be in reception ready to greet them personally. On a wedding day, the couple will be made to feel like VIPs. We want to give them a taste of that experience even before they have booked. Why not go one step further with a personalised welcome sign and a drink already poured and waiting for them?

## 3. START WITH A CONVERSATION

Almost every venue tour I have been on starts with, 'Can I get you a drink?' As lovely a gesture as that is, it means that, if I accept, I'm immediately left to sit and wait while you now disappear off to get me a drink. Instead, sit down with your couple right away and get to know them a little bit. This is your opportunity to hear about what they are looking for from their wedding day, any concerns they may have and what their dream wedding looks like. Take some time to build rapport and listen before taking them round the venue.

## 4. LISTEN MORE THAN YOU SPEAK

Your venue will sell itself – you don't need to fill the couple's heads with lots of facts. Instead, showcase the space (which you will have set up to look amazing) and let them digest it. Remember the information they shared with you earlier. Now is the time to weave that back into your conversation. Pick up on any concerns they may have and find ways to overcome them during the tour.

For example, if they are concerned about access for their elderly relatives, take the time to point out the lift or the quiet lounge space that family members can use in the evening if they want to have a comfortable chair away from the party. Show that you are listening and that this isn't just the same tour you reel off to everyone. Give the couple space to ask questions and to discuss their thoughts with each other.

Just like viewing a house, couples will either fall in love with a venue instantly, or they won't. You will be able to pick up from their body language and conversation which of these categories they fall into. If you want to give them the best chance of falling in love with your venue, you need to help them see the vision. In an ideal world, you would have your spaces set out as they would be on a wedding day. Most people need to see what's possible with their own eyes; they find it hard to dream. Have you ever looked around a house that is best described as a 'fixer upper'? They are trying to sell you the potential but, if you are anything like me, all you see is the peeling wallpaper and the holes in the carpet. I need to see the transformation, to know what's possible.

If it's not possible to have the space set up for a wedding, then have boards on easels in each room that showcase the space as it would look for a wedding, with key information also listed, such as how many people the space can seat. This is a simple, yet effective way to show people what's possible, even if you can't have it set out in front of them. If you want to go a step further, I have also seen venues use VR headsets or 360° videos so that couples can step into the virtual world where the wedding is set up and looking amazing.

## 5. FIND SOMEWHERE COMFORTABLE TO CLOSE THE SALE

Don't end the tour with the walk round. The final part should be a conversation with you, where you plan the next steps. Find somewhere quiet and comfortable to take them back to and find an excuse to leave them alone for five minutes. Now is the perfect time to offer to get them another drink or, if they decline, find a reason to pop back to your office to get some paperwork. They have seen and heard everything, so now you want them to have a couple of minutes alone to have a whispered conversation about what they thought and what they do next. They won't do this if you are sitting in front of them.

In the UK TV show Dragons' Den, the entrepreneur pitches for investment in their product or company and the 'dragons' either say no or make an offer. Once the offers have been made, they usually give the entrepreneur a chance to 'talk to the wall'. They want them to have a few minutes to digest the information, make a decision or talk to their business partner while the dragons aren't listening. When you leave your couple alone for a few moments at the end of the tour, this is their 'talk to the wall' moment, and it's essential if you want to proceed with the sale.

## 6. GET A 'YES', A 'NO' OR A NEXT STEP

Now it's time to close the sale or agree on a next step. This may be the moment you walk them through the costings if you haven't already, and an opportunity to find out if they have any more questions.

Once all of that is complete, it's time to ask the question: Would you like to go ahead and secure a date? At this point, you need to sit quietly and give them a chance to think and answer. If they say yes, you can proceed with the paperwork and financial agreements and close the deal. If they say no, you need to ask some follow-up questions. Just as I outlined in the 'sales call' section above, you don't want them to leave without an agreed next step. Never end with, 'Just go away and think about it.'

Ask further questions. Perhaps it's a definite no, in which case you can let them go and cross them off your list. Alternatively, it may be that they have a reason they need longer to think about it. It may be the first venue they have seen, or they may want to book a second visit and bring a different family member with them. If that's the case, you can agree some next steps with them and an agreed time to follow up. If you decide to hold the date for them, give them a limited time frame. Remember, with no urgency they have no reason to book, and you may be losing out on another sale for the same date if you hold it indefinitely.

## 7. FOLLOW UP IMMEDIATELY

Always follow up your conversation straight away with an email, outlining everything you discussed as well as the agreed next steps. This will help remind you of the conversation as well as being clear to them what's expected of them next. It's now down to you to follow the agreed steps to allow you to close the deal. For example, if you said you would call them on Monday, make sure you do.

## Final thoughts

As we close this chapter on sales, I have two final thoughts for you. First, whether the sale is a success or not, it's not personal. Some days I shop at one brand of supermarket, the next week I may visit a different one. I don't have a reason to hate supermarket one. They didn't upset me or do something wrong, I just decided to go with something different. If a couple decide not to book you this time, it's not personal. Review the interaction and then move on, you don't need to dwell on it. The owner of Burger King doesn't spend an evening sad on the sofa every time I choose to go and eat at McDonald's. Focus on the customers who do want to work with you. I promise they are out there.

Second, it's not a no until they say it's a no. I have heard stories of couples who have had sales conversations with a wedding pro and then have stopped replying to any emails, only for them to reappear six months later to say they still want to go ahead and sign the contract. We don't know what's going on in people's lives, so unless they tell you it's a no, or that they have booked someone else, that lead may still be alive. Follow up consistently and drop them a message from time to time with a simple 'Are you still interested or have you booked someone else?' It's not a no until it's a no, so just ask the question. They may still need you to solve their problem.

## Let's get practical

Every sales conversation will be different, and the more you practise, the better you will become. Give some of the steps in this chapter a go. Even if you don't manage to implement everything perfectly first time, making a start on one will make a difference.

1. Write down a list of problems you solve for couples and why your service is worth paying for.

2.   Review your last few sales conversations or venue tours that haven't led to a booking. Can you work out which of Zig Ziglar's five sales obstacles got in the way?

3.   Use the framework outlined above for your next sales conversation or venue tour. Can you walk away with a confident 'yes', 'no' or agreed next steps from the couple?

7

# RELATION-
# SHIPS

Being friends with everyone

When I was growing up, my dad taught me at a young age that life was all about *who* you knew and not necessarily *what* you knew. He was self-employed himself and would often be out at networking meetings and business breakfasts, building new connections. At the time, my sister and I would laugh and ask how going for breakfast with people could be considered work. His focus on connections stuck with me, and throughout my life I have seen how building relationships can lead to new opportunities.

When I was sixteen, the school explained that we needed to find a week's work experience. Most of my friends wanted to be teachers or to go to work with their parents, but I told my mum and dad that I wanted to work in TV. I'm sure many parents would have laughed and said it was impossible, but mine said they would see what they could do. One of our neighbours worked at the local news station and, after a couple of conversations, he managed to get me the go-ahead. I spent a whole week behind the scenes of the news set and I *loved* it. I also had my first taste of how a connection could give me an opportunity that I had dreamt of and, from that moment, I knew anything could be possible with the right connections.

As I reflect back, I can see how privileged I was to have these opportunities and to have access to my parents' connections. But once I left home for university, I knew that it was time for me to find my own path. Perhaps you had a very different upbringing or didn't have supportive people around you. If that's you, it's possible to start right now to build up your own connections.

My first experience of creating my own connection opportunities came in my final year of university. I was studying television production and I needed as much work experience as possible under my belt before graduating in order to have a chance of getting a job at the end of my degree. My favourite show at the time was I'd Do Anything where Andrew Lloyd Webber was trying to find the next 'Nancy' for his production of *Oliver*. As a huge musical theatre fan, it would be a dream show to work on. At this stage, most people would probably have parked that dream in the 'probably won't happen' part of their brain, but I was determined and I knew if I could reach the right people, maybe that dream could be a reality. I sat on my university bed watching the episode on my laptop and, when the credits started to roll, I hit pause. I started writing down the names of everyone on the production team and decided I would email all of them. The next morning, I set about sending my emails, every one of them asking for the opportunity to have a day's work experience on the show. I probably sent thirty emails. Almost all of them ignored me... except one.

## It only takes one yes

The biggest fear people have when building connections or seeking opportunities is rejection. We don't want to ask the question in case we don't like the answer we get. I encourage you to change your thinking and realise by *not* asking, you are always getting a no. When you *do* ask, there's a chance that you may get a yes. You don't need a yes from everyone – but when just one or two people say yes, it can lead to huge opportunities.

I sent thirty emails to the production team of I'd Do Anything. Deep down, I didn't expect anything back, but I wanted to ask the question, because I had nothing to lose. I got ignored by everyone, except one person. They replied and offered me the chance to go the following weekend for a one-day work experience placement on the show. I was thrilled to be given this opportunity and thankful that I had allowed myself to send those emails.

That work experience day was a dream come true. I made the most of every moment, spoke to as many crew members as possible, worked incredibly hard and was polite to everyone. I knew that I had one opportunity to make the most of this day and I wanted people to remember who I was. It paid off, and the next weekend I was invited back as a paid runner. I worked every weekend until the end of the season. That one yes gave me the biggest opportunity and was the start of my whole career in television.

## Wedding industry connections

I tell everyone that the wedding industry is the best industry in the world and I really believe it. Not only do we get to work on the best day of people's lives, we also get to make couples' dreams become a reality. The industry we work in is one of collaboration. It takes a whole team of different people to bring that one couple's day to life.

Our industry lives and breathes on connections and there is room for everyone. When I owned my wedding videography business, I knew that I needed to meet other like-minded pros in order to become known in the market. I attended as many networking meetings as I could to build relationships. When we relocated across the country, my local wedding industry connect count was back down to zero. I knew that it was down to me to do something about it.

*The wedding industry is the best industry in the world.*

I booked to attend a local wedding show to promote my business and, during the quieter moments, I started chatting with the other stall holders. I walked around the room picking up cards and asking if they would be interested in meeting for some networking drinks. The reception was warm and everyone was keen to meet up, so I got a date in the diary and sent the invite. That first networking night had thirty attendees and I had gone from knowing nobody in the local area, to having thirty new wedding industry connections. That thirty turned into three hundred, and now I have thousands of wedding industry connections across the world.

When it comes to creating your own industry connections, I am going to break them down into three categories, all of which are beneficial to your business.

1. Relationship between the wedding venue and the wedding pro

2. Relationship between two wedding pros

3. The 'competitor' relationship

## Building great connections

Before I delve into the specifics of each of these relationships, there are a few principles that apply to all of them. If we work on these elements, we will have better connections and relationships across every aspect of our life, not just within the industry.

### LISTEN MORE THAN YOU SPEAK

Have you ever met someone at a networking event and, before you have the chance to say hello, they have launched into a full pitch about themselves and their business? If you can't get a word in edgeways, you soon find yourself wanting to extract yourself from the conversation. Don't be this person! If you want to build deeper relationships with others, you need to get really good at asking questions and listening. The next time you meet someone new, don't launch into your life history. Instead, ask them about themselves first. They won't expect it and it will help them relax. After all, talking about ourselves is probably the easiest subject to talk about.

Ask questions to find out more about what drives them in business or what interests them the most. You can even ask them why they have attended the event you are at – perhaps you'll be the one who can offer them exactly what they are there to achieve. If the person you are chatting with is open to making a genuine connection, then eventually they will turn the conversation around and ask a question back, allowing you to share your business – without it sounding like a sales pitch.

When I worked in an office, I loved to get to know everyone – you never know when you can help each other out. There was one person who wasn't interested in chatting – the IT support man. He was known as the office grump, biting people's heads off when they asked him for help and generally just being a bit miserable. Most people rolled their eyes and gave him a wide berth, but I wanted to get to know him. I know how important it is to have the IT department onside when you have a technical meltdown. Over the first few weeks in the office, I tried to start a conversation when I came in or when we both happened to be at the tea stall.

Then I had a brainwave. I realised I needed to talk to him about something he really likes and feels comfortable talking about. My personal laptop had broken and I needed to get a new one but I haven't a clue when it comes to choosing computers. The next morning when we met at the tea station, I mentioned my broken laptop and how I wanted to seek his advice as he seemed very knowledgeable on the subject. The walls came down, and all of a sudden he was chatting away about the best laptops for my situation. In that moment, everything shifted. From then on we always had the odd conversation and, whenever I needed help with something, he was always happy to help me. All it took to build that relationship was to give him some time to talk about something he was interested in and to listen, rather than assume he was just there in the corner to help when I had a problem.

Next time you meet a potential connection, remember to listen, ask questions and be a good listener. You will find you build a deeper, more authentic relationship that will be long-lasting.

## TALK TO EVERYONE

We may work in a very niche industry, but that doesn't mean we can't find connections in all sorts of places. A few years ago, I was on a school trip and got chatting on the bus with one of the other parent helpers. We had never met before, and soon I got to asking him about his work and how he had managed to negotiate the day off for the trip. It turned out he owned a photobooth company. In the most unusual of situations, I had found a new connection. Two weeks later, he came along with his booth to one of my events and we have had a working relationship ever since. Imagine if I had avoided the subject of work? I would have missed the connection right in front of me.

Find opportunities to talk about what you do at every turn, but remember that the gentlest way is to ask the other person about their work first.

I once went to a business networking breakfast and got chatting to a television aerial installer. He was a lovely man, but my head couldn't help but think, 'This is probably not going to be a very useful connection.' But I asked him more about his work and in return he asked me about mine. I explained what I did and his eyes lit up. 'My partner is starting a wedding make-up business. Can I give her your details?' You really never know where your next client could come from!

## CONSIDER WHAT YOU COULD DO FOR THEM, NOT WHAT THEY CAN DO FOR YOU!

When we go into a relationship looking for what we can get out of it, we are going to fail pretty fast. We don't want to 'use' friends and business relationships purely for our own gain. If you start a conversation with that intention, it will be very obvious very fast.

Instead, remember my golden relationship rule: think about what you can do for them and expect nothing in return. This

*Think about what you can do for them and expect nothing in return.*

unexpected way of being stands out a mile, because it bucks the usual trend of being filled with self-interest. Although we hope to gain business down the line, being willing to help is the best place to start. When you are offering rather than taking, why would they want to say no?

Have you heard the saying that some people are drains and some are radiators? Don't be a drain and constantly take. Instead, come from a place of giving, just like a radiator – whether you're networking face-to-face or showing up on online spaces.

## Actively seeking connections

Now we have looked at how to build good relationships, let's look at those three types of connections you should be actively seeking.

### 1. RELATIONSHIP BETWEEN THE WEDDING VENUE AND THE WEDDING PRO

'How can I get recommended by a venue?' is probably one of the questions I get asked the most! This is the most complex of the relationships, so I want to tackle it first. A venue holds many of the cards. It usually makes up the largest portion of the wedding budget and, crucially, it is often the element that is booked first by the couple. Once the couple have booked their venue, they will often be handed 'the list' of recommended suppliers. If you are on the list, it can be a great way to get regular enquiries into your business. So how do you get on this elusive list? That is the golden question!

Venue managers and wedding coordinators are regularly inundated with requests to be on 'the list' and are usually far too busy and overloaded to respond. As with each of these relationships, when it comes to building a relationship with a wedding venue, we mustn't neglect the *relationship* aspect.

Why should a venue recommend someone that has just dropped into their inbox out of the blue? It's like someone dropping into your DMs to ask for a date when you have no idea who they are! The fastest way onto a venue's list is building a great relationship with the person who makes the decisions. So how does this happen?

Venues have more people who want to be on their 'list' than they have space for, so if you want to get one of the coveted spots, you have to stand out from the crowd. Remember to think about what you can give to them, rather than what they can do for you. Instead of asking 'Can I be put on your list?', let's think of ways you could approach a venue and help them first.

### a) Offer a service for free

I'm now going to contradict a principle I suggested earlier. This is the only instance when I recommend offering the service for free – and that's because it is a form of marketing and one where the long-term relationship could be financially lucrative. Of course, you need to have boundaries on how much you offer for free and you should continually weigh up the time you are spending versus the opportunity and financial gain.

As I have said that, let me tell you about an amazing saxophone player I once worked with who was looking to grow his business. He desperately wanted to be at more venue open evenings but didn't have much budget to pay to exhibit and was unknown by most venues. I recommended that he started to research who had wedding open days coming up over the next few months and to contact them. He contacted every venue and asked if they would like him to play at their event free of charge. He knew his live music would add to the atmosphere and give all of the guests a great experience. Why would the venues say no? That saxophone player got more bookings than he could cope with and performed at almost every venue open day in Bedfordshire that season. He was inundated with wedding couples who heard his music and made an enquiry, and his business became an instant success.

A wedding photographer I worked with noticed a venue was opening up near to them and he wanted an opportunity to be seen by them. The venue held an open event for local suppliers to come and look around, so I suggested they took their camera. There were plenty of photographers in attendance, but she was the only one who had her camera with her. She asked the owner of the venue if she could take some pictures, both of the event and of the venue itself. Of course, the venue owner was delighted to be able to use the images, and that photographer became the first person on the new venue's recommendation list.

### b) Offer to promote the venue

Every single one of you has a platform that can benefit a venue. Whether it's your social media accounts or a blog on your website, you have your own marketing tools. Why not write an article reviewing your favourite venue, or offer to interview them live on your social media? If you are offering to market the venue for free, why wouldn't they want to say yes?

Whenever you work at a wedding venue, remember that you are being watched. Work hard and be kind to everyone. The venue will want to work with wedding pros who are easy and not hard work. Be a great communicator, turn up on time and be efficient. Help the venue staff and be respectful and kind to everyone. I have seen plenty of wedding pros do their job but ignore the chaos around them, when they could have stepped in to lend a helping hand. If you make a great impression and everyone talks about how great you have been, they will want to see you back at their venue time and time again.

And venues, don't forget your pros! Although the venue holds most of the cards, if you work for or own a venue, you should not forget how important the wedding pros are to you. A great supplier team mean your events will run smoothly – they are also a great marketing resource. Word travels fast in our industry. Having a whole lot of wedding pros talking about how great you are in the local area will lead to more business.

As a venue, it's easy to build local relationships. People will be biting your hand off to be a recommended supplier. I realise time is not always on your side, so I recommend having open evenings twice a year where you invite local pros in to see your venue. This will lead to great social content and lots of new connections. It will also be a great way of showing off your venue while simultaneously showing your local pros how much you value them. Don't run events which are exclusive to your 'list'; always open them up to a wider audience. There may be some great people out there that you are overlooking.

## 2. RELATIONSHIP BETWEEN TWO WEDDING PROS

The wonderful thing about the wedding industry is that our ecosystem allows us to work together in a wonderful way. There are many elements that make up a wedding day, and each one of us plays a part. But we are not competing with each other – we are working together with a common aim. Growing your network of fellow wedding pros will give you plenty of opportunities to be recommended to couples and will inevitably lead to work.

There is an exercise I do in workshops sometimes where I ask wedding pros to picture a business in their head when I say the following categories: wedding DJ, wedding photographer, florist, cake maker, photobooth company, and so on. Afterwards, I ask for feedback and find that they all had particular business owners who popped into their mind.

I then leave them with this challenge: how many people think of your business when they hear the category that fits you? If you make wedding cakes, you want to be the first business your peers think of when a couple asks them for a recommendation. So how do we achieve this?

### a) Get to know more people

Just like marketing, connections is a numbers game. The more people who know about you and what you do, the more likely they are to promote you to their couples. If you want more people to know your business, you need to put yourself in the rooms where they are – both physically and virtually. The more curated the space, the easier the connections will be to make. Let me explain:

I have a free Facebook group 'Wedding Pros who are Ready to Grow'. There are people in there from all over the world. It's probably impossible for all of them to get to know you and your business unless you are showing up every week asking questions. Even then, it's unlikely they will understand the depths of your business.

Inside my paid online membership – the Wedding Pro Members Lounge – the relationships run deeper, the community is smaller and everyone has a common desire to grow their business. They also tend to have the same ethos as I do and are therefore open to lots of new connections. These business owners show up on calls together regularly. It's a safer space to ask questions, so relationships are formed and they often lead to referrals.

When I run an in-person event, relationships are supercharged. In my opinion, nothing can beat sitting down over coffee or lunch and talking with someone face-to-face. This is why any kind of occasion where you can meet wedding pros in person is always worth prioritising. Get yourself to conferences, workshops or drinks meet ups – and if there's nothing in your area, plan something yourself.

Five years ago, I met Adam at a conference I was speaking at. We were about two hours away from where I live, yet I discovered Adam was based only fifteen minutes from me. He was just starting out as a wedding videographer and wanted to know how to grow his business. He didn't have a huge marketing budget, so I suggested he needed to 'become known' and start building connections. I explained to him that, the following month, I was hosting a Wedding Pro Members Christmas party near to where he lived and that perhaps he should come along.

Adam took me up on the idea and turned up at the party. He knew nobody other than me and we had only ever had a fifteen-minute conversation. Adam threw himself into the event, chatting to everyone and making friends. By the end of the night, *everyone* knew Adam. He was a lot of fun and he had made himself very memorable. Guess what happened? Everyone remembered Adam and, every time a couple needed a videographer, they started sending them to Adam. Very quickly Adam became booked out; his business was transformed by that one event. Connections are powerful.

### b) Say yes to opportunities and show up

If you want to be noticed and make connections, you need to put in the work. Don't wait for people to approach you. You need to put yourself in the right places.

Look out for opportunities to be involved in styled photoshoots. A styled shoot is where wedding pros work together to create a wedding-themed photoshoot. The final images can then be pitched to publications and used for their own marketing. They are a great way to meet like-minded pros who have the same style as you.

In terms of finding opportunities, why not ask in my free Facebook group 'Wedding Pros who are ready to Grow' or plan one yourself? When you are exhibiting at a wedding fair, make the most of the quiet moments and talk to everyone else around you. If you have something to give them – cake makers, this is perfect for you – then this can go a long way towards making you memorable. If you are in virtual spaces, find reasons to show up and ask questions. Reply to other people's comments and go above and beyond to help people out.

You will never grow your network by being a quiet observer. Whenever you are pushing yourself out of your comfort zone, it will feel uneasy – but just like Adam showing up to a party alone, the benefits can often outweigh the initial fear!

When it comes to sharing contact details with other wedding pros, I prefer a proactive approach. Don't hand over a business card that they could lose or throw away.

Instead, connect digitally with an email follow-up, a WhatsApp message or a social-media DM.

## 3. THE 'COMPETITOR' RELATIONSHIP

'Are there any other DJs attending your event?'

I saw the message and replied, 'Yes, a couple of great ones will be there.'

The response came back, 'In that case, I won't be attending as I don't want to be in a room with my competitors.'

My heart sank. Why are wedding pros still thinking in this close-minded way? I am a huge believer in the phrase 'community over competition', which means that even the people who do exactly the same as you can be your biggest advocates, supporters and friends. A room full of other DJs wouldn't be a negative. In my opinion, it could be one of the best rooms to put yourself in.

At the first networking event I ran, I met Rachel. Just like me, she had a wedding videography business and we hit it off straight away. We had an in-depth conversation on cameras, the perils of editing software and details that anyone

*Community over competition.*

who wasn't a videographer wouldn't have been interested in. I knew in that moment that we could support each other and pass each other work that we couldn't manage ourselves. I could have thought of her as 'competition' and walked away – but, instead, we bonded, continued to support each other and are still friends all these years later.

Stop worrying about the competition. There's plenty of work for everyone. Think about how many weddings happen in your local area every single week. There's no way you could service every single one of them.

You should have a bank of contacts who do exactly the same as you! You can help each other move your businesses forward and recommend work on to each other when you are already booked. They can get you out of a hole if you become unexpectedly sick or have a family emergency.

If you receive an enquiry and you can't make the date, reply to the couple with recommendations of colleagues who might be able to help them – and let your colleagues know you have passed on their details. I'm sure they will start doing the same for you.

## How do you remember everyone?

It turns out I have the skill of remembering details about people and their businesses, months – sometimes even years – later! I have met thousands of wedding pros over the years, but I try and find things we have in common and it helps me remember who they are.

What should you do if this isn't your superpower? Let me tell you a secret hack! When you meet someone for the first time, connect with them on social media and send them a quick message.

Hey Tina, it was great to meet you today at Hatfield House for Kelly and Mark's wedding. Your flowers looked sensational and I hope we can work together again soon! Enjoy your trip to New York. I've always wanted to go there, Becca.

Now this seemingly simple message is doing a few things. It's putting down the details of who they are, where we met and one thing we have in common. If I come across Tina again in three months' time and can't remember the details of our conversations, I can go into my messages and be reminded of the info immediately. That means I can confidently pick up the conversation with her. 'I know it was a while ago now, but how did you get on in New York?' Tina will be amazed that you remembered, and that connection just got a little bit stronger!

What about the people who don't want to connect? I want to acknowledge at this point that not everyone has the same ethos as I do. The chances are that you will come across other pros who are less willing to help you out or who will see you as competition and not somebody they want to connect with. In life we can only control our own approach to life and business, and we can't often impact the views of others.

But I want to encourage you that there are plenty of amazing people in the industry, so if this is your experience, put yourself in different spaces and find the right connections for yourself. If you talk about your own ethos of 'community over competition', the right connections will make themselves known.

## Let's get practical

1. Write down a list of three venues, three wedding pros and three 'competitors' that you want to build a relationship with this year.

2. Research wedding industry events and online spaces that you can be part of and show up and make an impact.

3. Practise listening more than speaking. Come up with a few questions that you can ask people that will lead to an open conversation about their work.

# FACING THE NUMBERS
Becoming profitable

You can have the perfect business – but if it costs you money rather than making it, it's actually just a hobby. This is crucial. Without a profit, your business will be unsustainable and you could also start to resent the time you spend on it due to the lack of reward.

I have met countless wedding business owners who look very successful online, but when I get into the depths of their business, it's not a pretty picture financially. Many of them are working for much less than minimum wage.

## Take your head out of the sand

The first step to becoming profitable is taking your head out of the sand and facing the facts. I have occasionally run a workshop called, 'Is it a business or a hobby?' where I walk business owners through their finances, looking at the costs and profit of their business.

*If your business costs you money rather than making it, it's actually just a hobby.*

We talk about how much they are paying themselves and if they are saving money for taxes. On more than one occasion, I have found myself with a business owner in tears, because it's the first time they have looked at the reality of the business they have poured their life into. Each month they have seen money come in and out of their accounts, but they have been afraid to look at the reality and convinced themselves that they are doing better than they are.

In my session, they had to face the facts and it was a tough realisation. Despite the tears, this was exactly the outcome I wanted to see because facing reality is usually the turning point for change. That was the point I could start to help them face the facts and become profitable.

## Let's face your numbers together

Before I dive into the methodology, I have a gift for you. I am going to share with you the spreadsheets that I created for my clients to help them work out their financial situation. The spreadsheets and accompanying videos will help you input the information we discuss below. If you would like a copy, just scan the QR code below:

### STEP 1: ARE YOU PAYING YOURSELF?

When I first started in business, I was doing what I like to call the 'treat payday'. Instead of carving out money to pay myself in my business every month, I was instead buying myself a treat every time my account had a decent amount of money in it. From perfume to beauty treatments, I loved to treat myself – but it was not a proper payday for the number of hours I was putting into the business.

Imagine I gave you a new office job tomorrow and told you to work thirty hours a week and some weekends. At the end of the month, instead of a pay cheque, I presented you with a bottle of perfume to thank you for your work. You would be furious. Perfume is not going to pay the bills! I am describing the worst employer in the world, yet this is how you may be treating yourself.

From today onwards, I want you to start changing your system for paying yourself. I want you to come up with a number that you want to pay yourself every month. If you are just starting out, this may only be a small number, but it's important we start getting you in the payday habit early. This number can be as big as you would like. But later in this chapter, you will need to plan how you are going to bring in the income, so you also need to be realistic. Once you have your number, it's time to decide on your 'payday'. You can choose whatever date you like, but I would like you to set up a direct debit on that day where your chosen amount leaves your business account, lands in a personal account and becomes your pay.

When I first implemented this method, I was terrified I wouldn't be able to afford to pay myself in anything other than treats, so I started with a small direct debit of just £100 a month. The small act of paying myself meant

I could contribute to the family, look forward to a payday and know how much additional income my family would have every month, even in the quieter months of the year. Every few months, I upped the payment amount, as I realised it was possible and that the money was there. I kept on going until I got to the 'proper' wage I pay myself now and I plan to keep increasing it into the future.

## STEP 2: WHAT IS YOUR BUSINESS COSTING YOU?

The next exercise I want you to do is to work out how much your business costs you to run every year. Even if you don't take a booking in the next year, you will still be spending money out on your business, and I want you to look at that number now. Write a list of all of the expenses that come out of your business that don't relate to specific orders. Categories could include website hosting, subscriptions, training, marketing costs, wedding shows, directories, insurance, accountancy fees and much more. Once you have them all listed, add up your total across the year.

As you go through this list, it's a good opportunity to see if there are places you could save money or places where you need to invest more. Is there a monthly subscription that would be cheaper if you switched to annual? Could you renegotiate your insurance premiums to get the cost down? Do you need to review how much money you spend on marketing and aim to increase it?

## STEP 3: ADD EVERYTHING TOGETHER AND ADD A TAX CONTINGENT

Now it's time for some maths (or the spreadsheet can do it for you). Multiply your monthly salary by twelve to work out your annual rate and then add it to your expenses from Step 2. This will give you the annual cost of running your business, before you take any orders. At this point in the spreadsheet, it will give you a very loose tax calculation based on the UK tax amounts. Please note, this is not going to be accurate and is not an accounting sum. It is just a simple way to ensure you take into account the fact you will need to keep money aside for tax, because it's often neglected.

Once you have completed your first three steps, you will have your first total, known in my spreadsheet as the 'blue' number. Why not fill out the blue number below, but use pencil, in case it changes!

Salary x 12 (from Step 1) =

Total business expenses (from Step 2) =

Tax (approximately 20% from Step 3) =

TOTAL (blue number) =

Now we have your costs, it's time to start looking at how you are going to bring in money to your business.

## Who is your sales manager?

When it comes to enquiries and sales in your business, would you describe your approach as proactive or reactive? When our inboxes are quiet, it can feel like we are sitting around waiting for the ping of a message in order for us to make a sale.

When I worked in radio, the desks next to me belonged to the radio advertising sales team. There were six of them and they had a 'sales manager' who ran the team. Each month on the large whiteboard on the office wall, the sales manager would write the name of each team member and next to their name there would be a 'sales target' for the month.

Now imagine Kelly's June sales target is £5,000. By 15th June, the whiteboard shows she's only at £100. She'll be called into a meeting with the sales manager and asked to explain why she is so far from the target – and, crucially, what she is planning to do to turn things around.

Imagine Kelly turns round and says, 'I am sitting by the phone every day waiting for someone to call or email, asking to buy. But nobody is.' Would the sales manager smile, nod and see this as a perfectly respectable response? Not likely.

Instead, they'd develop a plan to follow up on warm leads, go out looking for potential prospects and boost marketing efforts. That's what drives sales. Not passively waiting for customers to appear.

For you, there won't be a sales team or a sales manager, so you need to become the head of sales in your own business. It's time to step up and be proactive. Write yourself a sales goal every single month and track it through the month. This number will look different for everyone depending on your market sector and the numbers you have calculated in the previous section. There is no 'perfect' number. Whether it's £500 a month or £5,000 per month, find the goal that's right for you.

When you get halfway through the month and realise you are not on track, make a plan, follow up and do what you can to hit that goal! Need the accountability? Share your goals with a friend, colleague or family member and ask them to keep you on track. Inside my membership, we get together as members on Zoom and talk about sales goals and targets every month, so why not join us?

When I started implementing this mindset with my client Sandra, I saw her perspective shift immediately. At the beginning, she was drowning in numbers and fearful that looking at them would show her that the business was not as successful as she had hoped. After a few sessions, I encouraged her to look at her numbers, and they were not as bad as she had feared.

Once we had the oversight, I started setting monthly sales goals for her to help her get to where she wanted the business to be. In the first month she was tentative. She wasn't sure about having the pressure of a number to look at. When she came back to me a month later, her entire face had changed. She was excited to talk about the numbers and the fact she had smashed her first goal.

Each month she has gone on to hit her goals. The whole way she looks at her business has changed. She's no longer afraid of the numbers, she's excited to see them grow.

Setting a goal isn't a way of putting pressure on yourself. It's a way to track your progress and celebrate your achievements. Even when you don't hit your goal, it's a chance to reflect on why that is and how you can implement changes to ensure you do hit it next month.

## Let's set those targets

Now you know how important it is to have goals, it's time to go back to the spreadsheets to learn how to set them. I've broken it down into seven manageable tasks for you.

### STEP 1: WRITE DOWN YOUR PRODUCTS AND SERVICES

Write down everything that you have to sell in your business. Because of the long timeframe often involved in weddings, I recommend splitting out 'booking payments' and 'final payments' into two separate lines. In our industry, you may take the booking in one year, and it may be another one to two years before you see the next part of the money, so it's helpful to split them out.

If your products are all bespoke, try and split them into rough categories or average payments to make this simpler. For example, 'two-tiered wedding cakes' and 'four-tiered wedding cakes' or '£1,000 wedding dress' and '£1,500 wedding dress'. Don't forget to add any other products you may sell into your list like 'prom make-up' or 'cupcakes at Christmas' or 'photography classes'. Don't worry about what you call them at this stage. This is just for your benefit.

Let's imagine you're a florist. Your list may look something like this:

1.  Booking deposit for weddings

2.  Final payment – bronze package

3.  Final payment – silver package

4.  Final payment – gold package

5.  Corporate flowers

6.  Mother's Day bouquets

7.  Wreath workshops

## STEP 2: LIST OUT YOUR PRICING

Once you have your list of items, put an average price that you are charging next to each of them.

1.  Booking deposit for weddings: £500

2.  Final payment – bronze package: £1,000

3.   Final payment – silver package: £2,000

4.   Final payment – gold package: £3,000

5.   Corporate flowers: £200

6.   Mother's Day bouquets: £75

7.   Wreath workshops: £80

\* Please note that I am not a florist and that these numbers are just an example so that I can demonstrate the concept. They do not represent how much I think you should be charging.

## STEP 3: WORK OUT YOUR EXPENSES

Earlier we talked about overhead costs in your business. Now we need to look at costs which directly relate to your orders. If you were a cake maker, this might include the cost of ingredients, fuel for delivery, the box you deliver the cake in, freelancers who are coming to help, etc. You do not include any wage for yourself at this stage because we already included that in our previous calculations.

Knowing the costs involved will show you how profitable each product or service is for your business. Let me show you an example:

A customer pays £500 for the cake.

You need to pay:

Ingredients: £120

Petrol to deliver the cake: £10

Cake box: £1

Total costs: £131

Therefore, this cake would bring you a profit of £369.

You need to work out this calculation for each of the products and services that you have listed. This helps you to work out the sales targets. You will also see which products and services are most profitable in your business, so you can focus on these more!

I once had a client that sat down to do this exercise with me. One of the services they offered was crockery hire. They would pay a freelancer to deliver and collect the crockery from an event. Once we added up the cost of the freelancer and the travel expenses, we realised the business owner was only making a £5 profit. The stress and organisation was not worth the £5 it made her. She decided then and there that she would only offer this service as part of the largest package and she would no longer take bookings for crockery on its own. She wouldn't have realised the amount of wasted time and effort that this service was causing if she hadn't looked at the numbers.

## STEP 4: SET THE TARGETS

Now that you have all of the information you need, it's time to set annual targets next to each of your products and services. If you use my spreadsheets, the maths will work on its own. How many booking deposits do you think you can take this year? How many final payments will come in? How many Christmas wreath workshop places do you hope to sell?

As you input the numbers and see the profit adding up, you have one main objective: the total sales target figure must be equal to or more than the blue number we came up with earlier. In other words, total sales must exceed total costs.

If they do, you are not only profitable, but you are profitable *and* paying yourself for the work you do.

## STEP 5: BREAK THE NUMBERS DOWN

Now you have your annual sales targets, I recommend breaking them down into quarterly and monthly goals. This is easier to track month to month.

*Total sales must exceed total costs.*

You could just divide them equally – but your business is unlikely to have the same pattern every month.

Use the knowledge you already have, alongside your marketing plan, to estimate roughly how the sales will fall each month. Perhaps you know you get a lot of booking deposits in February and March, but most of the final large payments come in June or July. Ensure your numbers reflect those rises and falls.

**STEP 6: KEEP TRACK**

Find the method that works for you when it comes to keeping track. I have clients that love a spreadsheet. They have a complex spreadsheet to track their numbers, with sales target vs sales made. I have others who have a large whiteboard that they update because they love seeing the targets in front of them every day. Perhaps you are a paper-and-pen person? Many of my clients track their annual, quarterly and monthly sales targets in my 'Undated Wedding Pro Planner', which you can buy on Amazon. Find the method that works for you and start doing it, every single month. It will have a hugely positive impact on your business.

## What if the numbers don't add up?

If you are struggling to make the numbers match, then you have four options:

- Decrease your expenses
- Decrease your personal salary

- Increase your product pricing
- Increase your sales targets

If your numbers don't add up, don't do nothing. Pretending it will all be OK is the fastest way to watch your business go under. Instead see this as the moment you take back control of your business finances and work proactively towards making a profit. Just give it a go and see what happens. You can always adjust things along the way.

## Let's get practical

1. Create your finance spreadsheets (or download a copy of mine).

2. Complete all the steps in this chapter to find your blue number.

3. Ensure your sales target is equal to or greater than your blue number.

4. Start tracking your numbers against your targets *every* month!

# FINAL THOUGHTS

We made it! I honestly never thought I would get to this point. Writing a book has been hard. There have been days where I wanted to give up, days when I doubted my ability and days when I was regretting the day I ever thought that writing a book was a good idea! But here we are. It's done. And, as we all know, done is better than perfect.

As you start to build your wedding business, you will probably go through similar emotions. Some days, you will question your life choices or consider throwing in the towel and going back to an office job. Keep going. Work through your to-do list and get the next task done. Your business won't ever be perfect – nothing ever is – but it is possible to make it a success and to be profitable in the process, so don't give up.

Whenever I doubt my abilities, I always go back to why I made a decision in the first place. With this book, I wrote it for you so that you could have an easy-to-digest, simple guide in your hand. If you make one change in your business based on what you have read, the hours of work I have poured into it will have been worth it.

Why did you start your wedding business? Did you want to get out of a dead-end job that you hated? Perhaps you wanted the flexibility of self-employment? Or maybe you just wanted to do more of the thing that you love? Whenever you have those moments of self-doubt, go back to that driving force and remind yourself why you are here. Look back over reviews that you have had from couples or the happy photos you have seen from the wedding day. Those moments make the hard work worth it.

I encourage you to look back over this book often. Grab a highlighter and scribble notes all over it. It's not a book to be read, pondered over and left on a shelf to gather dust. It's a guide to making progress in your wedding business – and keep making progress. There are ideas that you can revisit over and over again.

I know you have what it takes to run a profitable wedding business, doing what you love, so go out there and make it happen. Celebrate your wins and share your struggles. If you remember nothing else from what I have written, just remember this:

# DONE IS BETTER THAN PERFECT!

*Becca xo*

# WORK WITH ME

I have given you a huge amount of advice in this book to help you on your wedding business journey – but I know nothing beats the personal touch.

## ONE-TO-ONE SUPPORT

If you would like my eyes on your business and assistance developing a personalised sales and marketing plan, then get in touch about my one-to-one consultancy services. I take on a small number of clients each year. From accountability to step-by-step guidance, these sessions are designed to transform your business and set you up for success.

## SALES AND MARKETING WORKSHOPS

Are you looking for an in-person workshop for your team? I run these high-energy, interactive training sessions for clients across the world and I would love to see how I could support your business. I will take the principles from this book and bring them to life, leaving your team with a renewed enthusiasm, new knowledge and personalised goals. The sessions are built with your team in mind. Get in touch to find out more.

## THE WEDDING PRO MEMBERS LOUNGE

If you are looking for ongoing business development training, accountability and support, then my low-cost Wedding Pro Members Lounge is for you. This online membership community allows you to connect with like-minded wedding pros, learn from the best wedding business experts from across the world and stay accountable to me with weekly and monthly accountability check-ins.

## THE WEDDING PRO AGENCY

Do you recognise the need for more marketing in your wedding business but don't have the time or knowledge to make it happen? I set up the Wedding Pro Agency with you in mind. The agency can take tasks off your hands – from social-media posting to website updates, blog writing to email marketing, and more. Take a look at the Wedding Pro Agency page on my website to find out more about how we could support you in an affordable way.

Becca Pountney
becca@beccapountney.com
beccapountney.com

*Becca* POUNTNEY